Fragments

Fragments

Cool Memories III, 1990–1995

◆

Jean Baudrillard

Translated by Emily Agar

VERSO

London · New York

Published with the financial
assistance of the French Ministry
of Culture

First published by Verso 1997
This edition © Verso 1997
Translation © Emily Agar 1997
First published as *Fragments: Cool Memories III 1990–1995*
© Editions Galilée 1995

Verso
UK: 6 Meard Street, London W1V 3HR
USA: 180 Varick Street, New York NY 10014–4606

Verso is the imprint of New Left Books

ISBN 1–85984–891–5
ISBN 1–85984–123–6 (pbk)

British Library Cataloguing in Publication Data
A catalogue record for this book is available from the British Library

Library of Congress Cataloging-in-Publication Data
A catalog record for this book is available from the Library of Congress

Typeset by SetSystems Ltd, Saffron Walden, Essex
Printed and bound in Great Britain by the Bath Press

How can you jump over your shadow
When you don't have one any more?

After the best book, the most beautiful woman, or the finest desert you've ever seen, you tell yourself this is where the rest of your life begins.

In fact, something else happens: another book, another woman, another desert. And the rest of your life becomes life itself. It was merely the illusion of the end.

Even the hope of a definitive horizon, a horizon which would stamp what precedes with an irrevocable quality, is apparently not possible. New Deal of Life. New Deal of Desire.

If everything can seem indifferent when you have encountered the most beautiful of things, why don't we regard the opposite situation as equally fateful: having read the worst book, having seen the dullest landscape, having met the stupidest, ugliest woman? There should be a perfection of – and hence an absolute limit to – the insignificant, the useless, the trivial and the banal, beyond which, as in the contrary case, there would be nothing more worth waiting for.

In fact, it is not that way. After seeing the worst, you do not say, 'O time, suspend thy flight!'[1] There is no ecstasy of uselessness.

What powers saved my life? The powers of Good or those of Evil? Was it God or the Devil waiting for me at the bottom of the ravine? As in the illuminated manuscripts of the Middle Ages, I see these two forces fighting it out in the radiant skies above the Tautavel Gorges. As I am not dead, it would appear that God won. But perhaps the Devil victoriously interposed himself so that I could continue to do death's work?

What was apparent in the five seconds of the accident was not a question of life or death, but the issue of a clear or a cluttered future. When the impact becomes inevitable, you tell yourself: until now, things have been relatively simple. From now on, they are going to be horrendously complicated. You may even prefer death to that complication, that entanglement of causes and consequences. How is one to sort out this mess? Including the fact that one came out of it alive?

Just as the vital electricity of the storm seeds the earth, so the energy of the accident or the catastrophe trickles out over many years. For that to happen, however, you have to escape death – to practise *coitus mortalis reservatus* or the Chinese-style *post coitum mortalem*. But it is difficult to begin all over again every day.

What should not have happened did happen: the break-up. What should have happened did not happen: the serious accident, death. It is with such eventualities that one negotiates a vengeful, bitter intimacy – or a cynical complicity – with the course of things.

Above all, one must not believe in horoscopes. If he had believed in the one which predicted that he would live to be ninety, then the possibility of dying on a particular day, in a particular setting – not to mention, of course, the pleasure of not dying, of receiving the God-given supplement of the rest of his life – would all have been denied him.

If Venice, with its ramifications, its little alleyways, its interlaced spaces, could open out all its twists and turns like the convolutions of a cerebral hemisphere, it would occupy an infinite space. The equivalent, perhaps, of New York. And perhaps New York, by miniaturizing its circuits, could rediscover the labyrinthine charm of Venice. The one is the site of an indifferent antagonism, the other the privilege of a deferred death-agony.

The mathematical point through which the imaginary axis of the Earth's rotation passes.
The North Pole – the point where the wind comes always from the south, and blows always towards the south, since it is south in all directions.
The point where the compass itself can only indicate south, since, being at the absolute north, it can no longer indicate north.
The point where the meridians meet and where, consequently, it is every hour of the day at once.
The point where the year is encapsulated in an immense day, a single continual night: dawn, a single continual day, dusk.
The point where the stars neither rise nor set.

The point where the sun neither rises nor falls in the sky, but – in summer, when you can see it – revolves on the horizon at the same elevation.

The point where the Earth's centrifugal force comes to an end. At the absolute north, north no longer exists. Things can come only from the south. At the heart of the social, the social no longer exists. Things can come only from elsewhere. At the heart of the subject, the subject no longer exists. Things can come only from others.

All magnetic forces reverse.

For every point on the planet, there is no other direction than the antipode.

After the intellectuals partial to young flesh and those partial to dead meat, we now have the intellectuals partial to frozen meat, a thing neither dead nor alive, the flesh of concepts and ideas deep-frozen by artificial intelligence. Not to be defrosted – on pain of death (like freedom in Eastern Europe) – to be eaten as much as you like, if not more, and affecting all the signs of modish freshness, with all bacteria and all flavour (including that of dead flesh) removed. Just as the range of deep-frozen, fast-frozen foods gave rise to a new category of consumer, so this new mental substance secretes a new kind of predator, the jackals of the deep-frozen concept, the jackals of information and communication.

Neither dead nor alive ever again: this is the destiny of thought in the software freezer.

We have to give objects, including objects of desire, a chance to die violently. A vase, a chair, a book, a cupboard. Fire, breakage, disuse, oblivion. A chance to break inside your head and be smashed to smithereens.

These women who are unreal in so far as they are a fetishized part of myself. Hysteria of feminine projection, without which I would still be prey to that worst part of myself: masculine hypochondria.

When we had no means, we said the end justifies the means. Now that we have no ends, we say the means justify the end.

Neither is immoral.

What is entirely immoral is that there is no longer any contradiction between the two: ends and means have become indifferent to one another. They are quite simply no longer of the same order.

Everything works wonderfully, expanded like polystyrene, driven by the generic flows of the generators: the metastatics of Good.

Everything goes badly, all the circuits diverge, driven by anxiety and driven to anxiety: the erratics of Evil.

Warhol: reintroducing the nothingness into the heart of the image. 'It is only when all transcendent order has been denied that the questioning of the object and its limits becomes possible, enabling you to escape the aesthetics of imitation which governed the sensible world up to that point as a reaffirmation of divine power.'

Either you have not to be serious and seem it, or to be serious and not seem it. Those who combine being serious with seeming serious are insignificant.

The obsession with becoming slimmer and slimmer is an obsession with becoming an image, and therefore transparent, an obsession with the disembodied ideality which is that of film stars. Disembodiment is the price paid for immortality, extreme slimness being the only way to pass through death.

For a while now she has done nothing but make mistakes. Small mistakes, in her actions and decisions. Am I to take this as a sign (a bad one, clearly) or does it signify nothing at all? But isn't that even worse? What has no meaning does not even have the pure and simple innocence of parapraxes.

Telling any old thing to someone is to transform them into any old person. This is precisely what the news media do.

A pill against your house burning down.

Politicians of both Left and Right are equally useless. But those on the Left wear themselves out in finding a moral angle for their depression; they have not quite the measure of their real corruption. Whereas all-out free-market liberalism provides those on the Right with an insight that is fully equal to this depressed situation.

Having deliberately 'passed' on reality, he has the impression of being a particle of anti-matter lacking the corresponding matter, and hence the possibility of destruction. The highly specific melancholy of laid-off antibodies.

Animals are more alive than we are. They run off with greater vivacity, take revenge with greater tenacity. They obey or disobey with greater freshness and spontaneity. They are more cruel in their reflexes. From every point of view, and under cover of their voluntary servitude, they are infinitely superior to us.

French conceit goes so far as to claim that the Chernobyl cloud did not cross our borders. We are such a sanctuary of Culture and Human Rights (which originated in the true Revolution) that the lethal cloud from the false (Soviet) revolution could not reach us. No more than can international villainy: the Mafia and scandals happen everywhere else, but not in France. We do just about accept a few little natural catastrophes but, generally, Nature, which we invented in the eighteenth century, cannot be against us.

Eugenics and all its variants might perhaps be justified if we had the prospect of a higher race (but there is no race superior to man – such as he is, he is the absolute horizon of evolution, since he is the destroyer of the cycle). On the other hand, all genetic engineering aimed at moving the species towards a normal perfection – that is to say, a statistical mediocrity – is thoroughly despicable. Unless there is in this some obscure desire to obliterate the specificity of the species by genetic confusion. In which case, there is nothing to be said: human beings have always wanted to change the rules, at the risk of their own destruction. Until now, they did this in the symbolic order; from now on, they will do it in the biological order.

//
'If I could be sure that what I do is mere bluff, I would do extraordinary things' (Warhol). However, credulity is so widespread, it is hard to get oneself suspected. Everyone prefers to lend credence to reality, to sincerity, to the

honesty of writing. Even an entirely made-up quotation from Ecclesiastes receives official corroboration by the fact of its being published.

And indeed, what is the point of being an impostor? Everything falls back unfailingly into truth. Time itself conspires with truth. With time, any old imposture comes to be regarded as truth.

Yet the pleasure of being unmasked is all. But those who have tried to do this have not really succeeded. They have remained caught in the trap. Only a few know in what sense this is all mere imposture.

So far as intellectual 'work' is concerned, I have no idea about that any longer. What I have left is a total receptiveness in the void, where nothing is to be expected except from universal gravity.

Fragmentary writing is, ultimately, democratic writing. Each fragment enjoys an equal distinction. The most banal one finds its exceptional reader. Each, in its turn, has its hour of glory.

Of course, each fragment could become a book. But the point is that it will not do so, for the ellipse is superior to the straight line. It is also a matter of laziness: one has no right to waste time to no good end, any more than to exploit oneself to no good end. And a matter, too, of compassion for words, which have done so much work already.

By contrast with those who place all their hopes in the indigestion of ideas and arguments – the abuse of ideas, the prostitution of words and the textual harassment of language would be an interesting subject for debate – you will be judged on the brevity of your intuitions and arguments.

Another promise of fragments is that they alone will survive the cata-strophe, the destruction of meaning and language, like the flies in the plane crash which are the only survivors because they are ultra-light. Like the flotsam in Poe's maelstrom: the lightest items sink the most slowly into the abyss. It is these one must hang on to.

The nearness of happiness always reawakens the anxiety of puberty.

Tie me up. *Attami*. Fowles's Collector. Sequestration as the equivalent in love of hostage-taking, as the ultimate form of seduction. Seduction itself is a form of abduction [*rapt*], which entails a surrender, a violent complicity. The moment when she succumbs to the violence, obeys the cruelty which binds her, is the most intense moment of the love experience.

It is hard to imagine the reverse situation in which a woman would tie a man up or bind him to her in this way, except by sequestering him mentally.

Part her fleshy lips with a furtive glance. Keep them apart with a dreamy – or a spongy – hand. Linger with prophylactic caution. Bury oneself there with a spasm of derision. Be careful![2]

The little azulejo-blue calf, climbing the hill on a strip of blue carpet, which I slowly overtake on my caterpillar-track machine.

Unsexual ease – retinal chastity in a genupectoral position – trousers with braces.

The Unconscious, as they say, speaks. In fact, It [*Id*] exists only if you talk to it. It is like plants if you water them. It is something that is cultivated. If you forget it, it runs to seed. This is our agronomic culture of the Unconscious.

Gombrowicz, Nabokov, Svevo, Schnitzler, Canetti. How is it that the greatest are, in their varying degrees, violently hostile to psychoanalysis? And, ultimately, towards the end of his life, Freud himself?

Is it perhaps the case that Rossif filmed animals so well only because he secretly detested them? Everyone hides some measure of cruelty towards their object. There is no point in imputing this cruelty to unconscious motivations or some trite psychology: it is a symbolic rule. Analysis is part of the theatre of cruelty. Destruction is part of the (loving) understanding of the object.

What we are currently exterminating is not so much the human as the inhuman and the bestial – in man, too. Take, for example, the respective stupidity of man and pet in the consensual couple (dog, cat) and their sentimental duo – man keeping his whitewashed animality on a leash, in the shadow of the Humanoïdes Associés.[3]

My sign being the same as my ascendant, I am doomed to an obsessional coherence or a fatal dissolution. No disjunction, no contradiction: nothing there to counterbalance the omnipotence of sign and ascendant combined.

The one-legged man who leads a double life, hopping off elsewhere for his pleasure.

In their perpetual uncertainty – she of being loved, he of being desired; she of being appreciated, he of being wanted – they drifted bitterly apart.

That man who, for ten years, dined twice nightly, once with his mistress and once with his wife. Only once in ten years did they serve him the same thing: a *blanquette de veau*.

The only solution to the drugs problem is to make drugs a universal medium of exchange, the new general equivalent. That way, they would no longer be consumed. Shifting from use-value to exchange-value, they would become as abstract as gold or paper. You could store several thousand tons of drugs as international reserve funds, the way they do with gold at Fort Knox. For Gold Exchange Standard, read: Narcotic Exchange Standard.

Just as the Student of Prague rediscovered his image in the scattered fragments of the mirror, so the various singularities rediscover theirs in the broken mirror of the universal.

Two interesting situations: when thought moves faster than language and when language moves faster than thought. The worst thing is when thought and language move at the same pace. That is when boredom sets in.

Olfactory hallucinations. Not aggressive odours. A light but persistent nausea, for no apparent reason. With nothing of the delicious aesthetic vertigo of *trompe-l'œil* or the optical illusion about it. And why a particular smell of wood fires, of citronella, of damp? Whereas we happily accept that the mind can secrete mental illusions, it is scary that the body's machine can secrete material ones. The frightening thing is being physically fooled by your body.

There are two-way mirrors which allow you innocently to spy on people. This is one of the finest metaphors for consciousness. There is no two-way screen because there is nothing to see on the other side of the screen, nothing to see without being seen.

Revelation in a dream of a woman's treachery. Must I ascribe the responsibility for this dream to her? She certainly cannot be innocent. A dream doesn't deceive. The intelligence which arranges it is your own, but the passions played out in it originate elsewhere. It is awakening which restores the deceptive scenario of the sentimental illusion.

Along the same lines as Chuang-Tzu's butcher's knife: a blade as cutting as a glance. A blade so fine and subtle that it operates remotely. You have only to move it towards the lump of meat for that to fall apart on its own at the mere sight of the blade.

Coming back from the medical laboratory with the test results in an envelope, he posted them unthinkingly in the first letter box he came to.

The only people one really should detest are the interpretation professionals, the specialists in violence by insinuation, the intention-mongers and responsibility merchants. The critics, for whom every divergence betrays the author's sensibilities. The analysts, for whom every show of reserve is a mark of obscure resistance and bad faith towards oneself. The champions of artificial intelligence, who take you for temperamentally maladjusted (which is true) and look pityingly on you if you don't play their game.

All these sepulchral figures of journalism and the Paris intelligentsia in the TV studio. All with their tails caught in the ice, like Frans Hals's *Governors*.

To die by omission – a moment's lack of attention, and you no longer exist.
To kill oneself by absorption of the potential limits of existence.

By habituating yourself to it, you can take extravagant quantities of alcohol, just as, after many years, you can tolerate someone to a point that would be incomprehensible to anyone else. We already put up collectively with a level of crowding, sensory aggression and pollution that would be unthinkable to an observer from outside the human race.

Given that it is better to be killed by a bullet intended for you rather than a stray one, and given that there are many more stray bullets than ones which reach their target, is it better to be one of the terrorists or one of the victims?

Since I stopped having one, I have become very curious about other people's daily schedules. Whatever can they be working at from the moment they wake up? How can they bear having something to do from right after breakfast? How can they spin round all day long like fluid in a washbasin, until they reach the orifice of sleep? They tap away at the touch screens of their own lives, on which is perpetually displayed a hysterical daily round, and, from time to time, the ecstatic daily round of empty time.

Those whose time is gobbled up by useless activities cannot even conceive that you have nothing to do. You have to keep up their belief in this illusion, for they then accord you the same artificial respect as they have for their own all-consuming activity. By contrast with the other hysteria – that of slowness and boredom – the uninterrupted dynamism of business is merely the hysteria of dead time.

Modern activities have the same subtle function as scavengers in the desert: by devouring dead time, they leave pure time at our disposal. By putting an end to free time, they deliver us from the anguish of full time.

In the same spirit, we have to be thankful to the politicians who give their all to digesting the corpse of the political sphere – living sarcophagi who protect us from the rotting of a dead body which would otherwise invade the whole of society. All calamities protect us from something worse. Thus, the stupidity of critics must have a higher function – that of protecting us, by the thick layer of intellectual grime they secrete, from the secret violence of judgement which, without them, we would be forced to deploy, and turn round against ourselves.

It is the same with all those who deliver us from the wearisome obligation of managing money, business, leisure and morality. These are all superfluous tasks, happily devolved to the charlatans, predators and speculators, not to mention the waxen-lipped philosophers. Whatever we do, we must not try to correct the illusory nature of their discourse, since that would expose us directly to an unequal contest with stupidity, and with the burden of our freedom.

All these enterprises developing with no other purpose than the laundering of profits. All these building sites, doomed never to come to anything, which exist only so long as the subsidies, backhanders and speculation continue. All these projects whose sole *raison d'être* is enterprise and the moral imperative of performance like an artificial respiration. Whole lives devoted to facelifting activities, without even any aim of generating wealth or prestige.

Everywhere amnesties and the laundering of scandals, the laundering of fake bills. But it is not certain that the bill for this laundering, like the bill for the collective mind-bending that accompanies it, will not one day land up at the establishment's door. The media and the political class will pay dearly. They are already paying for the secured loan they have drawn on our advance of expectations. They have already lost all credence, all credibility.

There are still enough signs of the innocence of the world around us, enough signs of perpetual movement, chastity and malice, of lunar, autumnal, aquatic environment, to reawaken the imagining of primeval times.

There are beings whose beauty is heightened by a servile relationto someone even more beautiful, who in turn can do no other than devote themselves to a creature of even greater perfection, in an endless sequence.

Some have their wills, their lives, tortured by the fact of inhabiting a monstrous body. For others, the opposite is the case: the difficulty arises from the fact that they inhabit such a beautiful body that they can produce nothing equivalent to themselves.

It is indifference, natural or affected, which led him into this complex, dismembered system of a love life: never two women in the same place; if they became jealous or formed a friendship, the whole thing would collapse. It is that, too, which led him into this mental dismembering of the opposite poles of the will, rendering all decision-making strictly impossible. And also into the dissemination, the drawing and quartering of concepts, rather than a cosy life in the equivalent of the conjugal neurosis: the peaceful usage of basic concepts.

Why this paradoxical preference? The sense of drawing a certain energy from it, no doubt. But – most importantly – drawing and quartering, and dismembering, are forms of torture, and one can torture the intelligence just as one can torture the body and desire. And in these tortures one also finds a certain delight.

I have long wondered why my five flights of stairs are mysteriously more difficult to climb than other people's. There can be no doubt that they would be less difficult if I didn't live there, if I did not expect to find my double, whom I would really like to lose, at the top of them. I would like to slide in there like someone else, metaphorically slipping into someone else's shoes. And one of the charms of coming in late at night is the secret hope that the 'other' will have had the time to fall asleep, and you can slip between the sheets without waking him up.

All our societies on the verge of nervous breakdowns, but still they do not collapse. All these bodies subject to the most incredible physical, ideological, media persecutions, yet they resist with an improbable malleability. Far from bemoaning our fragility, we should admire our stamina and that of the social body as a whole.

All the useless frothing and occult swarming of the secret services have passed into the intellectual field with these thousands of conferences which now tail each other, not to speak of the double agents working for a foreign power, the power of virtual Stupefaction and comparative Unintelligence. With these thousands of researchers who, like false spies, have forgotten to take the price-tags off the soles of their shoes, just as they have forgotten to take the notes and quotations out of the presentation of their ideas. But you can still read the price when they cross their legs under the table, the brand names of their raincoats when they put them over their chairs and the vintages of their ideas when, with their fluorescent eyes, they squint beneath their glasses towards their conclusions, furtively wiping away a philosophical tear at their failure.

The Unconscious is like us, it is growing old. It is getting wrinkles and crow's-feet. You can recognize it, you can see it coming; it is itself acquiring neurotic habits. It is bowing to fashion, declining, dying a natural death. It has, in fact, already reached the ghostly state. Indeed, it is the same with the Unconscious as it is with ghosts: while their existence ought to haunt and disturb ours, we live without a thought for them.

God knows that if he were to show himself, he would cease to exist. He himself has never claimed to exist. He allows himself to be sensed only so that the problem of his existence may be posed. By contrast, advertising is much too visible and makes much too much play of its existence to be what it claims to be – namely, effective.

There is no more evidence of the effectiveness of advertising than of the existence of God.

Invocation seen on the pediment of a church: 'Que tienes que Dios no te haya dado?' What have you got which was not given to you by God? (implying: God gave you everything). But also: what are those things you have which God did not give you? (that is to say, those things which belong to you as your own). In other words, precisely the opposite. There is the same ambiguity in the line from the Bible: 'Without him nothing was created' [King James version: 'Without him was not anything made that was made']. In the Cathar version, this became: 'And without him the Nothing was created', which, in quite contrary vein, sets forth the principle of Evil.

There is never any chance of an essence reviving, whereas an existence always has a chance of a second existence.

The Frontierless: those who thrive on the absence of frontiers.
The Staphylococcus in the Phylactery.
The crystalline humidity of the full moon.
The final slaughter of mirrors.

Baudelaire says that every man bears within him a ceaselessly renewed dose of natural opium. There is, thus, an innate form of the will's dissociation from itself – secret element of birth. 'It is you whom your pipe smokes.' It is you the screen watches.

I suspect her of pretending to sleep to avoid any sexual contact. Only conversation excites her deeply, and her laughter ripples out while her words flutter around like speech-bubbles. But these bubbles [*phylactères*] are prophylactic: they protect her like gossamer.

The great condominiums being built under arc lights in the tropical forest of Puerto Vallarta: *de luxe* penitentiaries, elements for a final solution, like the refineries at Galveston or the Santa Barbara oil rigs.

The Swiss have recently – and hypocritically – denied themselves *foie gras* on account of the pain caused to the animals (the victim mentality has struck again!). They did not understand that *foie gras* was not a need but a luxury, a drug – the morbid consumption of the sick organ of a sacrificed animal, etc. One is reminded of *The Third Man*.

Switzerland is, indeed, a marvellous country: on the 800th anniversary of the city of Bern, the procession to mark the history of the city, made up entirely of autochthonous Swiss, paraded before an audience made up largely of Italians, Blacks and Japanese.

The charm of Switzerland is that hovering over this country – which is so comfortable, peaceful, monotonous and infantile – is the grandiose shadow of Nietzsche. All this *Gemütlichkeit* irresistibly puts you in mind of Sils-Maria. It is hard not to believe that all this *Untermenschlichkeit* is offered up daily – and will be for centuries – in expiatory sacrifice for the thought of the *Übermensch*, who paradoxically chose to emerge here, where all higher intelligence is immersed in placental comfort.

The trick of the Swiss was to provide the whole of Europe with mercenaries for centuries, and thus to be protected from war. The same trick is used by all today's rich countries which, by providing the whole world with weapons, manage to exile, if not violence, then at least war, from their territories.

The cities of Switzerland are the most squeaky-clean, the healthiest, the best-protected on earth, and even the old parts have such a brand-new air about them you would think they had been reconstructed, whereas they have in fact never been destroyed. Yet it is in these cities – Bern, Zurich – that the hardest '*öffentliche Drogenszene*' is to be found. Drugs are present everywhere, like the intravenous heroin of that wealth. The gold of the depths feeds the canker on the surface.

All these old ultra-Leftists thwarted (by History), unclear where they are on the Left–Right spectrum, and ending up writing with both hands – from left to right, of course – in the hope of one day painting spaces of freedom for themselves with their toes.

Rival advertisements for insurance companies. We assure you:
– from the cradle to the grave
– from the womb to the tomb
– from the sperm to the worm
– from erection to resurrection.[4]

Winter masochism of these thousands of women with naked legs and thighs in the freezing cold – a winter sacrifice which, by contrast, invokes a penetrating heat, every man dreaming of being the cold air which chaps their lips or the warm air coming out of their mouths. This lukewarm insinuation in winter of all the women who pass reminds one of *House of the Sleeping Beauties*. What a pleasure to caress a woman without waking her! Simply to be for her a paradoxical dream in which her body alone would find pleasure. What obscure desire in her to be violated without knowing it?

With every woman, one would love to possess her without her being aware of it, leaving her free to take her pleasure without our knowing it.

'[H]e was probably still capable of awakening her with his roughness. So he thought; but his heart did not rise to the challenge.'[5]

Boredom used to be born out of uniformity; today, it is the product of acceleration.[6] The more we believe we are escaping boredom by centrifugal force, the more we fall into true boredom, the frenetic *ennui* of particles and Brownian movement. Perhaps there is still time to play on the acceleration differential, to recover the inertia and boredom of which we are no longer the masters.

You can argue with the person who knows, you can argue with the person who does not know, but the Buddha himself cannot argue with the person who believes he knows.

Who are you then, J.B., you who speak of simulacra, but a simulacrum yourself?

Answer: it is because I exist that I can advance the hypothesis of the universal simulacrum and simulation. You who are already unreal cannot envisage the unreality of things. You who are merely the shadows of yourselves cannot advance the hypothesis of transparency.

Those who practise alterity or solidarity as a conjugal duty – or at times, indeed, as adultery – when they believe they have to betray their identity.

By a kind of creeping indecisiveness, but obscure remote control, I manage to skirt round decision-making and to surprise things by inertia. Basically, the only approach is to leave things to their natural inclination, which is to occur. This way, one always arrives at one's ends by a mixture of objective chance and weakness.

Expressions of respect and admiration merely leave one perplexed and disorientated. This is because one is robbed of one's defences by the impossibility of rejecting or answering them (with an equivalent sign). It is, then, like being paralysed by an insulin jab. Admiration is the intravenous form of aggressiveness. This is why it is so difficult to express or receive. If it is true that it is a passion, then its expression is of the order of the crime of passion.

Thomas Bernhard. Why this infatuation with a flabby blaspheming, entirely on a par with the flabby deflatedness of the age? His hatred of Austria is also on a par with that country: it is provincial. His spiteful parody of awards ceremonies (Wittgenstein) is as heavy-handed as the ceremonies themselves. He owes his success to the fact that he shamelessly shares all the characteristics of his age, including vulgar complicity with the object being denounced or parodied.

His cry? Poor Büchner, poor Beckett, poor Joyce, poor Genet! You can gauge the extraordinary self-satisfaction of this St Thomas in the Austrian-style cry, in the cry of the Philistine. The cry of the cunning gravedigger in a necrophagous opera.

His exile? He is not in any sense an exile in his society. He is, typically, the court critic and curser of a fat society whose heavy energy he sucks out to distil it into a conventional cry – the vaudeville of anger and hate. There is in him something of light comedy and Sacha Guitry. There is in him, quite simply, an impostor. And naturally, the infatuation of his doting admirers is part of the imposture.

We are used, particularly in art, to simulation *en abyme* (the copy of the copy, etc.). Thus, for example, Elisabeth D. literally copies Warhol's flowers. They sell as copies. And very expensive they are, too. From the aesthetic point of view, this is a total mystery. From the commercial viewpoint, there is no mystery at all. But what would flowers fetch if they were copied from Elisabeth D.'s by some unknown painter? Doubtless nothing. But they would perhaps regain value at the fourth generation. There would seem, then, to be a periodicity of simulation, and highly diluted simulacra would produce the same effects as the originals – as in the case of 'the memory of water'. Borges is supposed to have said: if you translated a text into another language, then back into your own language, and kept on doing this an infinite number of times, you would inevitably get back at some point to the original text.

Thanks to ultra-sophisticated meteorological computer programs, it is going to be possible to forecast the weather for the next day and the day after that without the slightest risk of error. The only thing is: the program will take four days to run. In four days' time, then, we shall know precisely yesterday's weather and the weather of the day before that. The truth about the weather [*le temps*] has no regard for time [*le temps*]. And the facts simply have to fall in with this. If need be, the truth will correct the facts retrospectively. It will have been fine, even if it rained. For facts are facts, but the truth is the truth. It always arrives too late, but when it has arrived, it is truth that commands belief.

One begins at a very early stage to fight against medicine and not against one's own illness. And in the end it is by abreaction to medicine and its terroristic, protectionist machinery that one is cured – and by that alone. In this sense, there is no evading medicine. It has perhaps inherited from witchcraft itself that perverse function of the abduction of ills.

The security guards patrolling the entrance to the Ministry are inclined to be tolerant while the (Gulf) War lasts, but they become inflexible once the dangers have passed.

It is normal for a function to become exasperated when it becomes useless. Bureaucracy, for example, has long been an exasperated (and exasperating) function. Advertising shows its exasperation in self-irony, anti-advertising and antiphrasis, having for a long time had no idea what function it is fulfilling. Sexuality shows its exasperation when its aims and purposes vanish (and desire increases when the effect recedes).

In the same way, antibodies become exasperated, unleashing autoimmune disorders, when they realize their uselessness in an overprotected body. They too, like the security guards, are salvaging their honour as useless extras.

In the recording studio, your thoughts parade as though on a teleprompter. You become the 'auto-reader' of your own ideas. Especially if you happen to glance at the monitor, where you see yourself talking in real time.

In a television studio, you feel your ideas emptying of their wit, of that kind of quality which one finds (if at all) only in a relation of seduction or rivalry. One is witty only in alterity, even if one has ideas in solitude.

Wit in this sense – the disturbing, surprising, charming effects of ideas – functions only within a dual, sensual game between minds. Something which the virtuality of the screen and of the millions of spectators prevents. The screen is a form of frozen, confiscated alterity – ideal alterity, perhaps, like the alterity of the Ideal City, in which there is no one.

In the satellite towns around Brasilia, which lies on a plateau that is supposed to be the world's magnetic centre of gravity, and in magical Arizona, its quartz substratum generating extraterrestrial vibrations, the human being everywhere invents cult places, cult objects, akin to cargo cults or Aztec sanctuaries, which are allotted the role of attracting the attention of a higher species of whatever kind. We are obsessed with the idea of being discovered, and live in fear of not being, or of having disappeared before it can happen. Biosphere 2 is a kind of mind-boggling preparation for that encounter of the third kind. Like messages launched into space or space modules loaded up with the emblems of humanity (Bach's music, etc.).

The Aztecs also lived in hope of encountering a higher race. But the Spaniards, when they arrived, exterminated them. Fortunately for us, no other race can be seen emerging on our horizon (though perhaps there is one emerging from within the depths of our own).

We are in a society of icy intolerance, where the slightest diversion from, the mildest breach of, the reality principle is violently repressed. Realist Philistinism and Pharisaism are triumphant on all sides. All ideas are immediately cast in concrete. The anathema level is the equal of any religious or Stalinist society. Nothing has changed. The conspiracy of imbeciles is total.

These fashionable spots where everyone recognizes everyone else without ever having known them. The voracity of faces, each lit up by the anticipated mutual recognition. Yet perhaps they did know each other in another world. This is the impression you get from Left Bank cocktail parties. Everyone has an air of *déjà vu* about them, and they float like shadows over the waters of the Styx. Moreover, hell must be just this: the compulsive remembrance of all you've been through without ever being able to put a name to a face.

The obscenity of the free zones, the tax-exempt zones, those frontier zones surrendered to the total vulgarity of commodities, is also to be found in the pedestrian precincts of modern cities. The extradition of the car ought to gladden our hearts. And yet we feel it to be an even worse farce, given the effort to fool us with the pretence of a city with a human face, whereas what is sublime about cities is quite clearly their inhuman character and, in particular, the vital alienation of car traffic.

When one looks at the emptiness of current art, the only question is how such a machine can continue to function in the absence of any new energy, in an atmosphere of critical disillusionment and commercial frenzy, and with all the players totally indifferent? If it can continue, how long will this illusionism last? A hundred years, two hundred? This society is like a vessel whose edges move ever wider apart, and in which the water never comes to the boil.

Little contemporary bestiary.
Protection – Zoos display an irresistible passion for the preservation of endangered species. A number of these are being protected, later to be released back into the wild. In the meantime, however, 'the wild' has disappeared! It is the same with human beings: ideally, they are recycled in human isolation cells (thalassotherapy, psychoanalysis, luxury health clubs, hospitals or asylums), and later released back into social life – in the meantime, however, the social environment has disappeared!
Reproduction – 'We have taken eggs from this tigress . . . These have been fertilized *in vitro* with the sperm of a Sumatran tiger and, for the moment, the embryos are being preserved. These should be reimplanted in a surrogate mother from a more common species, the Siberian tiger.'
Nutrition – What do animals die of in captivity? No longer having to find their food. So a replacement has to be found for this vital activity. With the big

cats, a chicken is hung up on a string. With the apes, the food is hidden in holes. With the birds, living insects are spread about . . . We are going to have to start doing the same for human beings. For what do they die of in society? Of a lack of vital activity, of no longer having to fight to find their food.

Transparency – people can no longer stand seeing the animals behind bars, so these are now being replaced by armoured glass.

Faces are increasingly becoming the pure substance of the image. As though there were a pressing need to fix this mirror of human passions in our memories before the tide of the inhuman sweeps over us. In this sense, the prostrate faces of the American prisoners on Iraqi television, faces with all the stuffing knocked out of them, remain the only images in the memory of that war that one can set against the techno-promotional flow of military operations.

Or, alternatively, the faces of the tennis players which television homes in on between the exchanges: in a state of cataleptic distraction, the player stares at his feet, contemplates his racquet as though it were a lost object; he no longer sees anything around him; he is in a phase of absolute affliction.

Not only do the journalists invited on to 'Caractères' speak of the (Gulf) War without the slightest doubt about its reality, in conventional, diplomatic and political terms, but they talk of their books as though they were pieces of supporting evidence. All they do is recite and reproduce them: this is what is called communication. Narrators of their own text, as though of a real object, without the slightest scruple. What contempt for the viewer, and for their books themselves. They merely rely on the journalistic exchange-value of their product, just as they merely rely on the political exchange-value of the event.

Storage of pleasure [*jouissance*] in the speculative circuits of capital (the Stock Exchange). Just as energy is stored in superconductors, with a view to recovering it one day. But isn't this, rather, a way of getting rid of it? The storage of pleasure is the pleasure of storage.

A table outside a café. A young woman is waiting. She has placed an advert and has an assignation with one of the respondents. In fact, she has a quite other objective: she is researching into the kind of men who reply to this type of advert. To avoid any misunderstanding, she will tell him as soon as he comes. The man arrives, and she talks to him. He replies that he himself is researching into the type of women who place this type of advert. In the end, the outcome is the same as it is with the personal columns. They end up falling into each other's arms.

Portuguese election poster: 'It's so good the first time, when it's done with love. Vote Socialist!' The poster shows a young couple arm in arm.
This is such crude manipulation that, like excessive make-up, it surely betrays a profound contempt. Here, the political class's contempt for itself. In fact, the erotic message conceals a real distress signal. All advertisements, beneath their euphoric externals, have something of this desperate tone and thus also, for those who are able to pick up the message, function clandestinely to deter. 'Don't vote for me whatever you do, considering how low I've fallen!'

The proof that the political class forms a parallel micro-society unrelated to *real* society and devoted solely to the task of reproducing itself is that the scandals which affect that class have no repercussions for it, just as financial crashes and scandals have no repercussions on the *real* economy, there being no relation between the two.

In a sense, this situation protects us: it protects civil society from the vicissitudes of the political class, just as it protects the economy (what remains of it) from the ups and downs of the Stock Exchange and international finance. This split, out of which arise a virtual politics and a virtual economy, is therefore to some extent beneficent. But in another sense, things are worse. For virtual politics and the speculative economy, on the one hand, and the real society and economy, on the other, are moving away from each other at extremely high speed, and will doubtless end up dying each in its own corner.

Memory is a dangerous function. It retrospectively gives meaning to that which did not have any. It retrospectively cancels out the internal illusoriness of events, which was their originality. But if events retained their original, enigmatic form, their ambiguous, terrifying form, there would doubtless no longer be any history.

The idea that an idea can be stolen from you is meaningless. If it can be stolen from you, that is because it is unimportant. If it can be stolen from you, the fact is that it is not yours.

Given the ritual of the cigarette after sex, we might wonder whether the latter is not destined to disappear when the former has disappeared. The simultaneous decline of the two is worrying. Might there be a causal relation here? In all those places where the cigarette is disappearing, a whole mythic culture of sexual pleasure, the cinematographic enjoyment of pleasure, is under threat.

Does the end of the great Empires also signify the end of the Empire of Senses, of Meanings, the Empire or Sway of Signs?[7] Does it mean we shall never again be able to do anything in the grip of [French: *sous l'empire de*] anger and passion?

Whereas the cinema is tending, rather, to disappear, dreams, for their part, are increasingly coming to take on an air of film. They are moving further and further from the primary process to become, as it were, post-synchronized. Thus, for example, I go so far as to film, in a later sequence, a passage which was missing from the preceding dream. Or else, if I don't like it, I intervene, *almost* with a sense that I am doing so (which does not in any way break the thread of the dream), in the way it is unfolding, or in the way it turns out. But what does it mean to say, 'if I don't like it'? Where has the objective dream-process gone? Unconscious, are you there? There was a time when you woke up to escape from a nightmare. Now, you correct the dream in the editing. Might not the alterity of dreams also be losing some of its power?

Change the facts of the real world. Instead of working uselessly on reality, bring to bear the mechanisms for switching between dreams and reality, the real and illusion.

For example: in a dream, our car is sinking in the river. I manage to get myself out and escape. But the woman with me is going under. I now have a choice. I can either act *in* the dream to save her, or act *on* the dream to push it in the right direction. I do, in fact, manage to do this: the dream changes course, and she is saved. I have only to operate on the dream as such to reroute its content (whereas, in the reality of the dream, I would have needed courage to achieve the same ends).

But from what point does one intervene in one's own dreams, from the inside, without waking? And from what point does one intervene in reality, from the inside, though without believing in it?

Disappearance of the memory of the dream at the moment of waking. The dream is there, so close, almost tangible on the screen of the retina, but it is impossible to grasp it. Where do the scattered atoms of dreams go? The wakeful man trying to remember his dreams is like a dead man trying to gather together his memories from life, or like a living one trying to remember the faces of the dead.

From the point of view of the dream, the passage into the waking state is like a death in which only shreds of the previous life survive. Perhaps animals also have these kinds of vague recollections which are immediately erased? A sense of returning, by the dilution of memory, to reptilian stupor.

Can you devote your existence to an idea which is not yours, or a woman you have never loved? I lived for twenty-five years with the University, that desireless woman, and I took my pleasure elsewhere. But how can you play the game for so long without being fooled for a single moment? What temperamental machine functions behind this split strategy?

You should never choose the ideal city or the ideal environment or the ideal woman since, if things fail, the responsibility is hellish.

Scandals serve as democracy's Tampax, when it has its period and the haemorrhage has to be staunched.

The cool, crisp feel of the pillow in summer is the cool, crisp feel of despair.

Working on the event as it happens, working in the heat of the event, as with the Gulf War, yet not in real time and not with the benefit of hindsight, but with the distance of anticipation. Journalism of the third kind, the very opposite of news reporting.

If commemoration is the soft form of necrophilia, the hard form is forced exhumation in order to establish a definitive autopsy. This is what those disciples do who track down and exhume all an author's writings, whether he wants them to or not. Excessive attention to texts is a variant of medical overkill. It is not too bad when it is the living who treat the dead as carrion in this way. The worst thing is the vulture who does it to himself while he is still alive, canonizing his least significant relics in advance, ensuring his own posthumous consecration.

Imagine the amazing good fortune of the generation that gets to see the end of the world. This is as marvellous as being there at the beginning. How could one not wish for that with all one's heart? How could one not lend one's feeble resources to bringing it about?
To have been there at the beginning would have been fantastic. But we

arrived too late. Only the end remains. Let us therefore apply ourselves to seeing things – values, concepts, institutions – perish, seeing them disappear. This is the only issue worth fighting for.

One dreams of a stealthy idea which would slip through all the detection sytems without being spotted, and unfailingly reach its target.

The subtle pleasure of arriving early and gauging, by the empty period which separates us from the precise time, what we are before we are there. But those who arrive late are doubtless also lingering over an equally perverse pleasure, having taken the time not to be there before they are.

Everything, before taking place, should have the chance not to take place. This suspense is essential, like the negative of a photo. It is this negative which enables the photo to have a meaning; it is this negative which enables it to take place – never the first time, always the second. For things have meaning only the second time, like baptism in anabaptism, like form in anamorphosis. Hence the fantasy that there will always be a second meeting, another chance, in another world or in a previous life.

There is never any definitive end to a relationship. All that has not been resolved, all that has not been said, must be there again in a second existence. It is in this 'reprise', as Kierkegaard would put it, that the deepest pleasure lies: that of vanquishing time by the play of the second meeting.

All essential events play a second time (death alone happens only once, and is not replayable). But this second time is also the last, and every event 'reprised', symbolically replayed, brings us closer to death. Once all events have been recapitulated in memory and cancelled by that evocation, one's destiny is sealed and the end is nigh.

I found her so beautiful in black only because I dreamt of her dead. In fact, it was because I dreamt of her as a widow. What I was in love with in her was the allegory of my own death. But I possessed that allegory physically – which is an original form of the work of mourning.

The individual is moribund –
But democracy is post-perennial.
Ecstasy is post-historic –
But the future is premature.
Jouissance is postprandial –
But silence is cerebral, etc.

With so much monotony that it isn't even clear that anything of the real conditions can be changed.
With so much torpor, it isn't even clear that you can push yourself to join in the show.
With so much reality, it isn't even clear that you can work the idea to the bone.
With so much communication, it isn't even clear that you can want to speak or write.

It is as impossible for the citizen to form an opinion on the basis of the news media as to form an aesthetic judgement on the basis of the art market.

When you think of the incredible neurotic complexity of millions of scattered individuals and the exponential sum of all these problems, you are aware that the psychical pollution of the planet is far greater than the biological or technological pollution. This certainly was not the case at Tautavel or Cro-Magnon. The short, fierce nature of life provided an automatic regulation. Today we have exchanged primary cannibalism for psychical cannibalism. We have moved into the stage of virtual cruelty.

The creeping inhumanity coming out of artificial technicity – the most direct emanation of the reptilian brain of the species?

Deafness is a lesser affliction than not being able to see. Because seeing is a constant marvel, and there is a sort of perfection of the visible. Vision enchants what it touches. Even ugliness becomes miraculous by the simple fact of sight, the eye, colour and the pure joy of appearances. Hearing is more visceral and dramatic, and hence closer to fear. Closer to language and meaning, and thus closer also to stupidity. For the absurdity of language is more penetrative, more poignant, more laden with meaning, than that of the spectacle and sight. This is why I would be more prepared to accept being cut off from the world by deafness, which spares us from its absurdity, than to be deprived of the sight of the world, even if the scene presented were an obscenity.

Hearing has more to do with the sexual, and deafness with sexual impotence, whereas sight and the gaze have to do with seduction. To live without seeing is to live without being seen – even if this does not prevent blind women from putting on make-up, and indeed doing so in front of a mirror. It is to live without seduction. A world without watching eyes is like a sleepless night, peopled with inner nightmares.

I have always wondered whether the blind can see and the deaf hear in their dreams. Do sight and hearing in dreams pass through the organs of perception? You can certainly fly in dreams without calling on the organs of locomotion, and you can talk without calling on the voice.

It is clear that deafness is the product of the obscure desire no longer to hear, to cut off the sound out of resistance to the harassment of the voice and messages. For the world is basically a wonderful visual reportage. It is the commentary that is unbearable.

In sinusitis, the swirling effect of your own voice inside your head. A feedback effect inside your skull which gives the impression of being bugged. Ideas themselves veer towards confusion for want of finding an outlet in the voice.

We speak of a veneer of intelligence, but use the term 'thickness' to indicate stupidity. What would a veneer of stupidity and a thickness of intelligence be like? Raised to the power of simulation, stupidity and intelligence merge. Every quality raised to the second power merges with its opposite. But stupidity remains superior to intelligence in that it is unintelligible.

The concepts of value, abstraction, speculation must be extended to cerebral matter, as they once were to the faecal matter of labour. Speculating on intelligence as grey matter valued like any other raw matter or material, with its equivalent in toytown money ... This matter is the prey of our headhunters now.

The successive immanence of objects beneath the structural policing of the gaze.

That which in the object is irreducible to objectivity.
That which in sex is irreducible to sexuality.
That which in language is irreducible to signification.
That which in the event is irreducible to history.

When you don't know what you want, you have to attach yourself to someone who does. Yes, but isn't the person who knows what he wants already suspect?
When you aren't sure of your own taste and judgement, you have to attach yourself to someone whose taste is sure. Yes, but, precisely, how are you to choose that person in those conditions?
When you aren't good at forming relationships, you have to attach yourself to someone who is. Yes, but how are you to find that person, and how are you to make contact if you are not gifted in that way?
When you don't know how to love, you have to attach yourself to some-one who loves you. Yes, but, precisely, how are you to make that attachment?

Information virus. A leitmotiv for the use of the Viral Disinformation Agency.

A communicable idea, thought, ideology, image, notion or concept, that is created by someone, for no one in particular but everyone in general, which purpose is to infect, invade, seduce, subvert, and ultimately transmute the host society, culture, metropolis centre, nation-state or any other system or cultural circuitry, seemingly on a self-propelling redundancy overload that is rushing towards its own collapse, destruction, annihilation, armaggedon and/or demise – This is itself an information virus designed to infect the immature host body politic.[8]

Will computers take us back to a material, inhuman form of intelligence? Will they connect back up with the destiny, with the general movement of matter, a moment interrupted by man and his history?

At dinners among intellectuals, there is a strong scent of subtle poisonousness, of gentle execution with buttoned foils, of chain-saw massacres. An intense energy runs through this ritual holocaust which for intellectuals takes the place each evening of the bloody conviviality of the Eucharist. The rest of the time is spent in resuscitating old titles, names, works and reminiscences, in defending the cultural potential against failures of memory. Amnesia or a lapse of memory on the part of one individual is contagious. Everyone else then loses the thread. The sudden forgetting of names and faces is as contagious as laughter. At fashionable gatherings it has to some degree replaced laughter.

The world ecology conference at Rio is part of the catastrophe. Montedison, a repentant predator, is financing ecological good works, such as the human race itself, on a global scale. In fact, the depredation is continuing through the measures taken to combat it: a hail of dollars falling on Rio which will, as usual, run off into the age-old channels of the Mafia and political power. To the physical, biological catastrophe are added the ideological disaster, the call to redemption and a global unholy alliance.

Where they get all excited about 'natural resources' and conviviality, I get excited about these pretty, translucent scorpions and nature's perverse design (unsurprising that they can take what I say only in homeopathic doses).

The Heidelberg scientists (a host of Nobel prizewinners!) assert that 'the state of nature does not exist and probably never has done since man made his appearance in the biosphere, in so far as man has always progressed by enlisting nature in his service, not the other way round'. In any event, these Panglosses have not progressed by enlisting the intelligence of nature in their service! Their proposition, aglow with the desire for scientific objectivity, amounts to saying that 'God does not exist and probably never has done since man made his appearance in the biosphere, in so far it has always been man who believed in God, not the other way round'.

The funniest thing, all the same, is this 'probably'. The scientific community 'asserts' that something has *probably* never existed! It is difficult to be more objective.

You can be the impostor of your own ideas (you don't believe in them; they have no effects for you) or the libertine (you treat them like dancing girls), the buffoon and the ham (you caricature them yourself), the militant

(you defend them zealously), the penitent (all militants end up in repentance). You can also be their naive accomplice and victim.

Most people become parasitic on their own ideas – when they have any. But, as it happens, these emotional attitudes also apply to those who have no ideas and who become, in succession, the buffoon, the militant, the penitent, the accomplice and the parasite of their absence of ideas, out of which they fashion a perfectly successful destiny for themselves.

Optimistic talk is clearly the most desperate, optimism being the psychological state which bespeaks the greatest uncertainty as to the existence of Good, and the greatest probability regarding the existence of Evil. If Good existed, there would be no need to believe in it, or to be optimistic (or, indeed, pessimistic). The two categories are equally depressive and pejorative.

That forgotten bottle in the cellar, which had perhaps been slipping a few millimetres each year, but was already protruding a few centimetres over the edge. It took advantage of the general indifference (the Gulf War, etc.) to continue its slide, and was not far from actually falling and smashing in a way which would have created one of those events that are insignificant but decisive for the very reason that, being purely accidental, they bear witness to a slowly maturing destiny and a blind will. But I saw it, stopped it in its tracks and put it back. As in that children's game in which the person seen moving has to go back to where he started from. But I know that it asks only to be forgotten again, and then it will resume its devilish project.

One after the other: the X-ray of my dustbins, the scanner portrait of my genetic code and the photographic inventory of the objects in my daily life.

In each case, a faceless analysis. The derisory mirror of your lost identity, your dejecta, the trifling detail of your life – forced identification, police-style investigation, as obscene as a urine analysis or a psychoanalysis, of which all these approaches are debased, technical variants.

General aestheticization of residues. Remnants of magic, the power of which was based on the arrangement of the traces and dregs, the nails, hair and dead particles of the other person. But what remains of the ancient spell?

I have dreamt of a force-five conceptual storm blowing over the devastated real.

American campuses. Like Disneyland, they are an ideal micro-city, the artificial ideal type of an intellectual biosphere. Like any realization of an ideal, they end up secreting a fierce coercion ('political correctness') and an internal intoxication, with its poisons and endorphins.

Epicurus: chance.
The Stoics: destiny.
The Sceptics: illusion.
The Cynics: irony.
Basic figures of ancient thought which have become heretical in the eyes of our modern – realistic and redemptive – thought, but are still as much alive. We have simply added two additional heresies to them: the principle of Evil and that of perfection (the Cathars and Manichees).

Suddenly, the arteries of memory seem severed. The opposite of phantom extremities, in which the absent limb seems still to have its nerve contacts. Here the objects are indeed present, but they are no longer innervated. Though visible and tangible, they are merely a memory, like someone close to you whose very name you cannot recall.

The presenter furious at my refusal to take part in his programme acts as though I were there, asks questions, waits, leaves a silence and says on the radio: There you have it. B. is here, but he does not wish to reply. Is this what you call a philosopher?

Pole position of death.
Last man into the scrum of organic conflicts.
Symbolic referee of the match.

The beauty of the dead when they are laid out on their sides. Not with their faces upturned to the sky – a sign of annihilation and Last Judgement – but on their sides, their legs tucked up, as a mark of foetal coiling and of sleep.

Whether an organism dies a natural death, or perishes because it carries within it from the outset genes and cells whose function is to put an end to it, are very different things. The latter is an automatic programming, without which life itself, the living organism, would be immortal. Without this specific, inhibitory action, life would be incapable of stopping on its own; it would proliferate to infinity.

Is it not the same with sleep? And with thought? Does it not take one agent to trigger this process and another to stop it? There certainly are inhibiting agents which intervene to halt the chain reaction of thought. Otherwise, it would dissipate into the void, into madness, into immensity, just as life would dissipate into immortality.

Our present pathology is one of the failure of these inhibiting agents, opening on to a prospect of exponential development of all functions.

In the Andean valleys of the Altiplano, the Indians live as though inside their own transfigured bodies. The rock there has the substance of flesh, and the colours – ochre, green and black – these oxydized, pastel shades – are the colours of the insides of the body, of the mucous membranes, of organ stereoscopies. Not to mention the pathways – the deep cavities, the clefts and faults in which they walk and move as though inside a body, but a body torn and open to the skies, retaining the initiatory and fleshly quality of a blood system. Some forms indeed bear fleshly resemblances to living matter – recumbent women, the rocky anatomies of flayed bodies, their tissues and veins coloured with metallic pigments. It is the Indians' fate to work in the mines, to extract that metal which shows at the surface of the rock, as it is sacrificially to extract organs from a body. A difference here from the North American deserts, where the same geological developments do not bespeak the same visceral presence or the same sacrificial ritual. They are the site of a more superficial, unreal, disincarnate delirium – being also admirable in their way. On the Argentinian Altiplano, it seems that God himself and nature itself have become the bloody metaphors of our own bodies.

Four axioms for an algebra of thought:
– the attraction of the void by the periphery.
Anti-density, anti-gravity. Jarry.

    – the equivalence of the beer and the cigar, the harmonious equivalence of non-being. Brecht.

    – the complementarity of being and its opposite, of fascism and anti-fascism, etc. Benjamin. Collusion between contraries.

    – the reversal of effects and causes, the precession of effects over causes, of the ends over the origin. Predestination. Metalepsis.

    A touch of gout
    A touch of arthritis
    A touch of wind
    A touch of asthma
    A touch of bronchitis
    A touch of athlete's foot
    A touch of long-sightedness.
    And, from the psychological viewpoint:
    Solidly temperamental.

    Oxymorons: a glimmer of despair – an *élan récessif* – the non-praying mantis – virtual reality.

    Aphelion: we are as far as possible from the sun.
    Apogee: we are as far as possible from the earth.
    Apathy: we are as far as possible from suffering.
    Mortal agony: we are as far as possible from death.

    What is the meaning of this trend towards writing in pairs? If the concept is – as it should be – an all-out adversary, if what is going on is a philosophical challenge or duel, then this has to be confronted alone. If we are talking of a piece of intellectual labour or research, then two – or more – can do it.

27 July 1992. Birthday. 63 years old. Exactly Doctor Faustroll's age at birth. An extraordinary coincidence: everything I am writing at the moment – about the Agency, the Transfatal Express, objective irony – has a Pataphysical dimension to it.[9]

The points-based driving licence is an excellent formula. But it is scandalous that this outstanding idea should apply only to behaviour on the roads. It ought to be extended to the whole of existence with the creation of an existential licence along these same lines. For every offence against the moral legislation on behaviour, you would be docked existence points. When you had used up all your points, your licence would be withdrawn. In this way, the highways and byways of existence would be safer and, moreover, less crowded, once all those who did not know how to behave were removed. And they would not, in fact, then have any occasion to behave well or badly any more since, by definition, unlike what happens with the driving licence, the withdrawal of the living licence would be a definitive act (the only way round it being to lead a double life). Some consideration might be given to providing a second chance by way of a process of retraining conducted by conscience experts who would reinject a respect for behavioural norms. In that case, people would be put on provisional survival. But the best solution, none the less, would be to have the life ban enforced immediately. You would only need to embed the points-based licence into the body as a kind of programmed implant to have the recalcitrant liquidated by automatic seizure.

This would be the unconditional application of Human Rights. And we should then have a clearer conception of the just and unyielding application of democracy.

1948: *The Best Years of Our Lives*.

The characters in the film have retained a candour towards – and naive faith in – their feelings which we no longer possess. Our feelings, which we delightfully term *emotions* in order to salvage the fiction of an *emotional* life, are not affects any more, merely a psychological affectation, having lost all credence in our eyes. Or, alternatively, they are conversion emotions, betraying the melodrama going on in the body rather than the nuances of the soul. We do not even have this candour in our relations to our dreams, where we grapple with their interpretation, their splitting, their ironic reflexes. But the worst thing is that not just life, but cinema too, seems to have lost all simplicity since that period. It knows only how to parody itself affectedly, and has veered towards psychodrama or visual melodrama. Retrospectively, these were then, also, the 'Best Years' of cinema.

Montjuich, July '92. The opening ceremony of the Olympic Games. The international tenor sings to the royal box. On the left, there is a giant television screen, on which he appears in close-up for the 120,000 spectators. As he cuts too small a figure in the actual surroundings, all faces are turned to the screen to see him. As he becomes aware of this, he too turns towards the screen and sings facing his own image. But then, given the camera angle, he is shown in profile on the screen. The spectators in the stands then immediately turn back towards where he is standing in flesh and blood. No one is looking at anyone else [*l'autre*] any more.

This is the 1992 version of *Las Meninas*, as seen by Foucault. The play of gazes in the classical age becomes gazes put out of play in the (tele)visual era.

We should plan to build niches filled with explosives into the buildings of the future, niches carefully distributed so that the buildings can be automatically destroyed at the required time (like the cells programmed from birth to produce death).

For an alterity without veils and an identity without scruples.
For an identity without veils and an alterity without scruples.

The entire political class infected by the contaminated blood affair. The virus moves even faster round the superstructures of power than it does round the victims' bodies. Basically, corruption and scandals have no effects on the political class, since it is immunized against real society. But that scandal is an original one, because it breaks down the wall which separates political from civil society, and constitutes an event on account of the invisible contamination – a viral event, for want of social violence, which is no longer capable of constituting an event.

'How can he describe such abominations? And how come he doesn't collapse under the weight of the abominations he describes?'
Well, it takes exceptional fortitude – or, alternatively, a special form of cowardice. At all events, you have to be abominable to come to terms with abomination. You have to collude with evil to be able to speak evil. You have

to have sold your soul to the Devil to be able to speak of the Devil (and doubtless also to be able to speak of the soul).

A kind of moral law, of terroristic superstition, denies you the right to speak of anything whatsoever if you are not involved in it. You have no right to talk about the Communist Party if you are not a member, no right to talk about psychoanalysis if you are not an analyst or being analysed.

Hence the equally terroristic corollary: if you analyse the system so well, then you are in cahoots with it. Caught eternally between two accusations – of corruption or imposture: 'You talk about seduction, you are merely a seducer'; or 'You talk about seduction, but you don't know anything about it.' Either 'You are in cahoots with the object you speak of' or 'You don't know what you are talking about.'

In fact, speaking of something and being part of it are two quite different things. The finest example is death: you have to be alive to talk about it. But this is true of anything – of politics, economics, art. You have to be a stranger to something to speak about it in a strange – that is to say, original – way. You have to be a man to speak of the feminine. All those who speak from 'experience' speak in a conventional way – they relate their life stories.

In fact, you have absolutely to collude in what you are speaking about and at the same time to be somewhere else altogether. You have to love it and hate it. You have to be the thing you speak of and to be violently against it. This is the law of hospitality, and it is the law of hostility.

The helots against the elites.

Those who have the privilege of being able to speak also have that of saying no, an act whereby they express their critical consciousnesses. The silent majorities are, by contrast, doomed to say 'yes', thereby expressing their consensuality and servility. On this occasion, in the referendum on Europe, it is stupidity which says no. For once, the whole of the political and media class, the whole of culture and the elite, are on the 'yes' side. Have they lost their critical privilege, or are we to believe that the masses are showing a transpolitical intelligence superior to the critical intelligence of the intellectual establishment? This result is a significant event because it reveals that what is in play is not a Right/Left political divide, but a more deep-rooted discrimination – between the 'clerks' and the clones, between the elites and the helots.

There have been tremendous efforts to show that the negative vote was politically brainless and inept. Perhaps, but given the brainlessness and ineptitude of the political sphere itself, the 'no', by an opposite effect, constituted a remarkable transpolitical act.

The political is no longer the defining aspect of History. History itself is no longer the defining aspect of our actions. As it is played out today, the political is merely a blackmailing by History and by historical Reason (which is always invoked when Europe is under discussion). In this sense, the negative vote is a 'no' to political blackmail, a 'no' to the arrogance of the 'European' political intelligentsia, assured in advance of the passive conformism of the (bovine) masses. This referendum would never have been set up without the contemptuous certainty that the people would mechanically follow the elite. But that is where the credulity of politicians regarding the stupidity of the masses far outstrips the credulity of the masses regarding the intelligence of politicians. It is through this dysfunction, this disaffection of every representative system, that unexpected convulsions become possible – convulsions no longer driven by a political *prise de conscience* but by a form of transpolitical abreaction against a background of radical indifference.

Or, alternatively, a form of political unconscious which would have rediscovered the paths of the negative (which was denied to it by Freud, for whom the unconscious could not say 'no'). The ultimatum delivered to stupidity has, in this way, turned around against the very people who issued it. The power of this unpredictable 'no' has a virus-like effect; it is a kind of leukaemic solvent running through the bloodstream of the political class. In the void of events which seem to be events, this really is an event. Not that it overturned the course of things, since Europe got through. But it was the first unpredictable event, emerging from the depths of polls and statistics, attesting to a society totally divided – not politically, but with regard to the symbolic exercise of speech and power. The first emergence of a blind rejection of the illusion of the political, a rejection of moral and political Reason, unanimously assembled on this occasion in its cultural, intellectual, media niche. The caste concerned, which has always possessed a monopoly of Enlightenment, naturally saw in this blind rejection merely a conspiracy of imbeciles, which had to be smashed by all available means: blackmailing them with calls for national unity, which in all other cases it condemns; imprecation; media brainwashing; and, last of all, contempt for universal suffrage and the denial of its own principles (the Danish 'no' is regarded as invalid, and we shall not even mention the quashing of the Algerian election results in 1993). Such is the difficult process of learning to respect human rights, which may also involve the unconditional removal of those rights. The democratic dictatorship is shaping up nicely.

Europe – the very archetype of the contemporary event: a vacuum-packed phantasmagoria. It will have taken place neither in heads nor in dreams, nor in anyone's natural inspiration, but in the somnambulistic space of the political will, of dossiers and speeches, of calculations and conferences – and in the artificial synthesis of opinion that is universal suffrage severely orientated and controlled as a function of the cunning idealism of leaders and experts.

It is a bit like the simulation, deep in the desert, of the Capricorn One expedition to Mars: Europe as virtual reality, to be slipped into like a datasuit. This, perhaps, is the perfection of democracy.

Psychoanalysis regards dreams as the realization of desires from the preceding day. But it would be so much better if the preceding day were the realization of the desires of the dream; for the movements of an unbound, free-floating illusion are richer than those of a reality under surveillance.

Not to think any more. To be like a dog. To be in one's head like a dog in its kennel.

The characteristic of the lymphatic individual is to be tired before beginning, but in great shape at the end.

The characteristic of the pusillanimous individual is to see his mind shrink on contact with the body.

The characteristic of the weak mind is to see his ideas shrink on contact with words.

Boredom [*ennui*] is a subtle form of filterable virus, of fossilized tonality, which might be said to pass invisibly across the substance of time [*la durée*], without altering it. Fine particles of boredom striate time like neutrinos, leaving no trace. There is scarcely any living memory of boredom. This is why it can superimpose itself on all kinds of activities, even exciting ones, since it lives in the interstices.

A scar on a woman's face lends her all the charm, all the attractiveness, of the animal which might have inflicted that wound (Canetti).

One must free oneself from one's ideas in writing, not take charge of them. One must free language from its purpose, free concepts from their meaning, free the world from its reality – which is an even greater illusion.

The worst thing when your ideas are plundered is the fact of being taken for a wreck.

It is better to be a victim of ostracism than to become an oyster-shell oneself.

The only outright success in a lecture comes when you throw the audience back on to their own devices: 'It's your problem!' Nothing makes people laugh quite so much as role reversal.

There is no need to attack politicians. They are engaged in spontaneous self-destruction. You simply have to be firm about not going to their aid.

'Liberated' East Berlin exports to the West its sexual promiscuity, which thrived in the shadow of dictatorship, and consequently AIDS too, in the form of a contingent of unregulated prostitutes. The West, by contrast, exports its stereo-video-porn to the East, the image and simulacrum of sex, of which those in the East were cruelly frustrated. This is more like a mental AIDS. In this way, the two cultures contaminate each other reciprocally after the fall of the Wall of Shame.

Artificial Intelligence inevitably produces an Artificial Intelligentsia, a body of intellectually correct, genetically immunized experts, which re-forms around numerical intelligence data and the digital mastery of the code.

We are reliably informed that – according to the reports coming in from all our agencies – the sun did not rise this morning. It is now 10.15, and the daylight expected at 7.30 (solar time) has not yet arrived. This unprecedented delay is not due to an eclipse. Might it be due to a slowing-down of the Earth's rotation? The scientists we have contacted have been unable to supply any explanation. We shall update you hourly with any new information, and most particularly, of course, with news of a sunrise, which we hope to see shortly.

One of our correspondents has suggested the hypothesis of a slowing-down not of the Earth's rotation, but of the speed of light. If that speed had diminished appreciably overnight, the sun would not rise. If it continued to decrease, there would be prolonged night over the Earth, for as long as that slower light took to reach it. The gradual slowing-down of light would bring us to the end, or at least to the redefinition, of the traditional sun.

Every woman must in a previous life have had a mercenary, a jester, an intellectual, an announcer, a lamplighter, a surveyor, and so on. It was perhaps the same man in the course of his metempsychoses and successive lives. For every man has also doubtless once been a jester, a serf, a mercenary, a butcher, a lamplighter, an air-traffic controller . . .

She sucks at her words as they come out. She seems to practise a constant fellatio on the words she pronounces.

At last an original humanitarian initiative: a support committee to allow Bosnian women raped by the Serbs to be given abortions. Even anti-abortion campaigners would be forced to agree to this. Even the Pope (though he denies nuns on dangerous missions the use of contraceptives). And yet, even then, there would be no end to the ambiguity. For, ultimately, 'therapeutic' abortions could easily veer towards ethnic cleansing.

An unknown individual accosts me outside a café: 'Surely you're not going to wait till you're dead to be loved?' The implication of his remark: when are you going to do what you have to do to be loved? Implied beneath this: you are not loved. Hurry up and die: it's your last chance.

But in another sense, the question suggests that I have to be loved one way or another. And that is also a declaration of love.

Neurotic and erotic abreaction in every place marked out for discourse or for writing: libraries, conferences, 'round tables', examinations. A desire to climb the curtains and swing from the chandeliers as soon as the discourse of culture makes its appearance.

If only stupid words could leave a material residue! What evidence of general stupidity!

To the north of Lisbon, a duel between a motorway under construction and a trail used by dinosaurs. A track 90 million years old against today's highway, which clearly will not last as long. What would a fossilized motorway look like? The dinosaurs win: the motorway will be diverted. Once upon a time, the dogs barked and the caravan passed by. Today, the fossils bark and the caravan halts. The traces of the dinosaurs howl in our memories. Had they been alive we would have exterminated them, but we respect their traces. It is the same with the human race: the more we imperil it, the more we meticulously preserve its remains.

Under the heading of everyday atrocities: the daughters of Moscow *apparatchiks* buying up on the black market from the Mafia the foreign travel scholarships granted to the irradiated children of Chernobyl.

By contrast, the ants imprisoned in an art performance at the Venice Biennale are set free by a court order after an action is brought by the Animal Protection Society.

Not much snow this winter. Without snow, the resorts become the mere ghost towns of an old sporting cult dating back to a glacial age. Imagine seaside resorts deserted by the sea.

So the *pistes* are made up with artificial snow, providing a *real* basis for a simulacrum of leisure. Suddenly, the real snow seems to take on an artificial dimension; it seems now to have lost that spontaneously unreal aspect which gave it its poetic quality. The artificial use of snow inevitably finds its counterpart, sooner or later, in an artificial snow. We could even imagine satellite snow-bombing, or an automatic snow 'unroller': you would slide along on your own personal strip of snow, which would be automatically 'wiped' behind you, like a magnetic tape. Is this not already the image of our real time, of our virtual reality – a short, programmed sequence of space–time in which an individual performance unfolds?

The carbon gas produced by all the winter tourist industries is contributing to the warming of the atmosphere, which is bringing milder winters and, as a result, an absence of snow and, consequently, disappointment among the masses who had, however, thanks to those same industries, seen a rise in their standard of living and, with it, increased chances of being able to take a skiing holiday.

The height of irony: these same holidaymakers, deprived of snow in the resorts, find themselves halted by snowdrifts on the drive home.

A terrorist act like the one that brought the Boeing down on Lockerbie produces an irresolvable dilemma. Either one chooses to stress the operational capacities of the terrorists and, as a result, magnifies their image, or one puts everything down to an accident or a technical fault. But this latter solution is perhaps even more catastrophic, for it is an admission of the failure of the system itself, and every accident then assumes the guise of a terrorist act.

In everyday life, there forms between us and others, particularly our nearest and dearest, a web of predictability which may be a residue of affection or hatred, but which we cannot escape. We ourselves confine others in this same captive imagination, obliging them to live in a particular future. We have our place, and it is extremely difficult to disappear. The ultimate trick is to be secretly at home when everyone thinks you are elsewhere, or to slip from the field of vision with the collusion of chance. It is as good as seeing without being seen, which is better than looking into a mirror and not seeing oneself there.

'Perdu de vue'[10] is a reality-based detective series. Apart from revealing a prurient urge to search people out, track them down and report them to the authorities, the programme shows up the fact that we no longer have the moral or civil right to disappear. But its success doubtless also derives from the fantasy of the millions of virtually nonexistent people whose only hope is to be refound and thus, for the duration of a programme, to be lifted out of their insignificance.

Simultaneously, my memory lapses increase, I forget names and faces and yet I am struck by flashes of resemblance and every face I meet begins to look like another or several others. This is surely all connected, but I fail to see how (another lapse).

One day at the Pointe du Raz, on the rocky plateau looking out on to the Baie des Trépassés,[11] the erratic tourists move around, far apart from each other, like contemporary stand-ins for shipwrecked souls.

By contrast with the cosmic evolution of matter, which seems to pass from the wave state (the first phase after the Big Bang) to the gaseous, and then to form liquids and solids, our social mechanics, the mechanics of the masses, seems to move from the solid (our primitive notion of the mass is of something solid, compact, and inert) to the liquid (the mass of flows and networks, a fluid, viscous, floating mass), and then to the gaseous state (the mass of even higher dilution, an intangible substance, scattered, infinitesimal in its density, but one which still makes up the main part of social matter, just as the scattered, gaseous mass makes up the main part of cosmic matter), to end up as a pure wave form, where the very concept of the mass disappears. In short, the social concept of the mass in a sense travels a path opposite to that of cosmic matter – from solid mechanics to wave mechanics, from matter to total immateriality.

Tautological, promotional blackmail: '100 per cent of those who won the Lottery tried their luck!' A slogan which people immediately reinterpreted the other way round to fit in with their desires: '100 per cent of those who tried their luck won!' (When they were interviewed about this advertisement, they none the less thought it went a bit far – no doubt by analogy with those elections where a hundred per cent 'yes' vote is a suspect result.)

The stratagem is easy to understand. If, in the effort to convince people, you tell them: 'If you want to win, you have to try your luck', then you have lost before you start. No logical, conditional proposition has any chance. On the other hand, by reversing the order of the statement, which has now become unconditional (winning is trying your luck), you create a kind of circular demonstration into which desire rushes all the more willingly by virtue of the fact that it is quite devoid of meaning.

Tautology, being the most vulgar logical expression, is always the strongest argument. It is like symmetry, which is so satisfying because it is the most impoverished, most visible form of order. Symmetry and tautology are self-evident; they impose a kind of visual equation: A is A, $0 = 0$. This is why their power of suggestion is immediate and total. Reflecting themselves in themselves, they function as mirrors of a perfect reality. Hence the fact that tautology is prophetic and most prophecies are tautological. Advertising rhetoric itself is tautological in essence. Hence also a family resemblance with ventriloquists (Ubu's belly echoes itself) and with those autistic children who excel at mental arithmetic and the memorizing of dates: we know they don't have time to calculate; the result comes up on their mental screens (and computers, for their part, function like autistic machines).

Ernst Jünger's hero, the hero of general mobilization, was the Worker. Our hero is the hero of general demobilization: the non-worker. When an unemployed man set fire to himself recently, his ashes should have been buried under the Grande Arche, as a counterpart to the ashes of the Unknown Soldier beneath the Arc de Triomphe. But what could they have used as a flame, other than the one in which he burned himself to death?

They ought to put up monuments to the Unknown of all categories: the unknown striptease artiste, the unknown TV viewer, the unknown air-traffic controller, the anonymous alcoholic, etc.

The unemployed man burning himself to death – the Neuilly terrorist slain by the GIGN – Bérégovoy sacrificing himself – Fabius, asking unsuccessfully to be sacrificed – Mitterrand already dead without realizing it. Death comes in a rich variety of forms these days.

Nature is merciful: when the drive or pulsion weakens, its remedy is compulsion. When the impulse falters, it substitutes repulsiveness. When passion fades, its remedy is compassion.

The communication function is closer than any other to the anal function. Not only does it absorb differentiated matter and reject the undifferentiated – the faecal matter of information – but, thanks to it, the relational field dilates and contracts like a sphincter. Excess of communication corresponds to a collapse of sphincters.

Perfection of language: the word 'inexorable' is itself inexorable. Materially, physically, phonetically – by the rainbow sweep of vowels which, in its cadence, describes an implacable curve – each syllable peels off irrevocably, culminating in the chiasmus of the 'X', between the high nasal and the unvoiced liquid.

With any material whatsoever, there must be a poetic resolution which encompasses and integrates all the fragments of a finite whole – one merely has to find the rule which organizes the reversibility of the slightest details, as in the poem – anamorphosis and anagram of all the fragments – so that there is nothing left over. Everything must have its place, everything must have its end.

The labour is never one of accumulating coherent facts, but of setting out from an arbitrary set and positing that that set, such as it is, is the best. Like the world, but not in the sense of the 'best of all possible worlds': there are no possible worlds; there is only this one. Just as it is, it is the best, just as the rules of chess are the best ones possible. Precisely because they are arbitrary, there is no obstacle to their optimal functioning. The rule of thought is of the same order (and is therefore formally opposed to all the rules of operation of the real).

With writing, it is the same as with everything else: you have to be quicker on the draw than your shadow. It is a kind of reflex act, over before it has begun. And it leaves no traces (when it is done successfully). Because it is, in a sense, the object that does the work. Because things find their articulation all on their own. But the price to be paid for this kind of automatic writing, this sort of effortless progression which brings into being something entirely self-evident, is an increasing difficulty in acting. It is not true at all that experience in writing or speaking makes these things easier. It makes them more and more agonizing.

The heretical bias towards indifference: that of the masses in social terms; that of concepts indifferent to their reference or their consequences; that of events which are insignificant, or indifferent to their historicity; ideological indifference to any cause whatsoever. Only language is not indifferent; only language should not leave us indifferent.

A dream. Trees, stumps, entire trunks, pass horizontally across the sky, twisting in an aerial flow of motionless wind. They pass down the sky, as they would flow down a river, branches breaking up and floating around like wreckage. The trees – some sawn down, others uprooted – seem like refugees from a tornado. Everyone witnesses this phenomenon, but no one is really surprised.

If the Left collapsed the way it did, falling far lower than its actual decline would imply, this is not because it is incapable of governing or because it has committed fatal mistakes (unfortunately, it merely committed a string of banal ones), but because, in spite of its advanced historical decalcification, it was not capable of coming to terms with the indifference and inertia of the social body. In a sense, it is almost to its credit to have fallen, not for having renounced its ideals, but for not having managed to rid itself of them definitively.

For its part, the Right identifies spontaneously with this inert phantom of the social body and its deep resentment of the political. In this sense, it is not so much political as transpolitical – that is to say, aligned with the lowest common denominator of a society that is politically closed down. It is, therefore, the Right which profits by this closure. But it, too, has no political perspective, and in this respect Left and Right have failed equally.

The most scandalous inequality is the inequality in the ages people live to and, therefore, in the length of retirement. Some enjoy twenty years of retirement; others don't even get to retire. Within the framework of a rational redistribution of the nation's incomes, should we not, at the appropriate time, give everyone a check on their life expectancy, and establish retirement schedules as a function of their presumed chances of longevity? Fixing everyone's retirement date in terms of the anticipated date of their death (established by all the sophisticated means we shall soon have at our disposal) on the basis of a retirement of equal length for all, thus abolishing one of the greatest injustices of democratic society.

Some idea swimming in the blue gelatine of the reptilian brain, seeking out the gossamer-thin difference between illusion and the real.

MAY 1993

Everything makes sense in the reverse[12]

Max Ernst paints a garden. When he has finished the picture, he sees that he has forgotten to paint a tree. He immediately has the tree cut down.

Admitting in confession, after years of silence, to a theft which had obsessed him, even though it was a trivial one. Having finally found the courage to speak of it, he is given such a banal penance that he loses his faith.

The history of the kleptomaniac translator: all the jewels, chandeliers and other objects of value disappear from the text he is translating.

Apophatic is the term applied to a theology which seeks knowledge of God through what he is not rather than through what he is. A kind of negative theology. One might envisage an apophatic history, which would start out from events that did not take place. An apophatic reading: the reading of a book in which one would come at the central idea from the questions not raised, the answers not provided.

The Perfect Crime, the Radical Illusion, the Excess of Reality, the Continuation of the Nothing: the pleasure of shaking those branches to which the last readers are still clinging.

In spite of all instances and events – travel, illness, romantic or depressive moods – the same idea presses forward, as though by remote guidance from within. It is frightening, yet at the same time comforting, to think that it would have worked itself out the same way in any other different circumstances.

Destruction of the neuronal flora by ingestion of media products which have passed their sell-by date even before being put into circulation. Destruction of the intellectual flora by the massive ingestion of conceptual products, sterilized or artificially preserved, like stereotyped political language, using bactericides, fungicides and anti-eidetics. Destruction of the linguistic flora which, like the destruction of intestinal flora, produces verbal diarrhoea, a disruption of digestion and something like a cacolalia, a coprolalia which has to be curbed by numerous pataphysical brainwashings.

The cyclist's swaying. It is true that you travel faster and more easily with a slight swaying motion, than by moving forward in a straight line. The bicycle confirms the curvature of space, and that of the body, which steers a course more direct than the linear.

With dreams, we have the fantastic experience of a reality in the pure state, with effects of mobility, emotion and mastery the like of which reality itself is unable to produce.

Starting out from a fragment of knowledge or a literal memory item, dreams are capable of producing a psychological perspicacity, a reading of others and their mode of thinking which is far superior to the knowledge we have of them in reality. I can remember bringing other people to life in my dreams and making them speak better than they would have done themselves, can recall having been for a moment a particular other person more than I was myself – reflecting that person, so to speak, from within. A strange state of receptivity, in which scenes and faces seem to come from elsewhere, whereas it is we who are wholly in charge. It is like glossolalia, when one finds, miraculously, that one can speak an unknown language with effortless mastery.

Dreams are generally seen as processes in which consciousness is altered by an absence. But might there not be processes of alteration by excess? Unhooked from himself and his waking consciousness, can the human being produce effects more intelligent than himself? This is what is claimed for computers: isn't their fantastic level of performance down to the fact that they are disconnected from all human consciousness?

Fifteen years later, upon being prompted almost by accident to do so, I experienced the resurgence of a foreign language which I had seemingly forgotten, but which resurfaced apparently spontaneously with its particular turns of phrase and subtleties. A fantastic situation! Unfortunately, the same rule applies as with Egyptian mummies: once they've been dug up, they very soon begin to decompose.

At last an African on the podium in the World Athletics Championship at Stuttgart! Africa surely deserved that reward! Fantastic hypocrisy, while most athletes mounting the podium are Blacks. But, by virtue of slavery and colonization, it is the USA, Britain and France which claim the title of great sporting nations – and are moved, in their lofty arrogance, at the 'exceptional' success of 'the little Namibian'.

The zealous enemies of stupidity have forgotten that it is both the illness and the vaccine, and that you have to have been inoculated with it to be able to exorcize it. And because it is extraordinarily contagious, you can't rage against it without falling into its trap.

A special mention must go to second-degree stupidity, that stupidity which has already turned around upon itself and come out on the other side, reinforced by a whole sophisticated and ironic critical apparatus of intelligence and culture.

True compassion is to suffer in silence for others.

In the cemeteries one finds only artificial flowers. But the villages are collapsing under the weight of natural flowers, as the cemeteries once did. Indeed, they now look like cemeteries, deserted as they are by both man and beast, yet knee-deep in flowers. And, beneath their perpetual festivals of bloom, they have become as squeaky-clean as funeral plots.

The end of our life is the supreme book
Which we cannot close or reopen at will
One would like to keep the pages one likes
But already the last of them is slipping from our grasp.

One can imagine a high-definition democracy, in which they would show the human rights chart every day, in real time on the screens, in the way they do now for the weather. They would show the observance and violation of those rights over the whole planet, possibly with immediate penalties (which would obviously produce a constant worsening of the situation).

The stupidity of all commercial or cultural anti-Americanism. As if Americanism did not run through every society, every nation, and every individual today, like modernity itself.

The clownish faces of our movers and shakers.

Even in the daytime, a part of us is perpetually asleep. When we are fast asleep, part of us is constantly awake. This is how, even when we are asleep, we can wish for sleep. How, even when we are fully alive, we can want to live.

The erotic striptease of those red trees of the Alentejo, stripped of their cork like skinned animals. Apart from what remains of the bark on the trunks and branches, like fur muffs on a smooth, bloody skin. Their beauty is on the borders of the vegetable and the animal, the human and the mineral, smooth as muscles and red as mucous membranes or coral polyps.

God exists, like the bottle-rack, since Duchamp has met him/it.
All those who believe they exist because they have met themselves take themselves, like this, for God or for bottle-racks.

Better the gentleness of uncertainty than the brutality of self-evidence. In any event, the latter is never sure either. The most striking signs – such as those of fidelity, for example – may, in any particular case, be interpreted the opposite way, since they are produced just as well – and even better – by infidelity.

Noble energy cannot be transposed into vulgar energy. You can run yourself into the ground in your everyday activity, yet you will not have expended that portion of noble energy, that accursed portion which will remain in you like an unpunished crime.
But vulgar energy cannot be sublimated into noble energy either, yet it must find an outlet. It too must have a secret destination (like the 90 per cent of useless genes). Perhaps, in the end, it is the true 'accursed share'.

The compulsion to repudiate those things which are close to you: family, children, country, nation. As though you had to disown what is given to you – for fear of having to give it back? To keep a prophylactic distance from one's own – but first from oneself, one's own name, one's own body, one's own face.

You gauge the flow of time only through others, whose faces are much fairer and crueller mirrors to us than our own image. This is doubtless because we recognize them through all their changing appearances, while one never recognizes oneself: one always rectifies one's image by reference to an ideal face from which one's present face is merely an exception – and never a definitive one.

The axons of memory are clogged up with the same kind of mucus as the bronchial tubes. Lapses of memory increase in direct proportion to lung deficiency.

The anxiety at any kind of commentary, even a favourable one, comes from the obscure sense of the skeletons in the cupboard, from the fear of seeing them emerge and suddenly show one up as an impostor or a criminal.

The ridiculousness and mediocrity of what is dearest to our hearts, of the person we are for better or for worse, which we have turned into a solid bulwark for ourselves, including in our writing. If someone sees through all this, you can be wrecked.

While I am lying next to a woman sleeping, another one beckons me, drawing me from the bedroom into the corridor, then into the street, where an entire erotic fantasy is played out without the sleeper's knowledge. Suddenly, the light goes on in the bedroom, a sign that she is awake and knows I am there, very near, in the company of another. All this happens in silence. Now, the woman I met outside is the same as the one in the bedroom. In my dream I know who she is. When I wake up I do not know any longer.

The mouse scuttling about in the rain between the points as the trains thunder by, making their apocalyptic din. Will the human race be capable, in fifty or a hundred million years, of surviving in conditions so lethal and absurd? No doubt it will, since the lethal transformation it *has* achieved took a few thousand years.

Today minimal energy is expended in work, while we deploy our maximum effort in leisure. The idea of reducing working hours is, then, to allow people to expend their energy in their free time. A health measure, so that those now disabled at their keyboards can work off their tension in body-building.

Copacabana. Thousands of bodies everywhere. In fact, just one body, a single immense ramified mass of flesh, all sexes merged. A single, shameless, expanded human polyp, a single organism, in which all collude like the sperm in seminal fluid. The lack of distinction between the town and the beach brings the primal scene more or less directly into the public arena. The sexual act is permanent, but not in the sense of Nordic eroticism: it is in the epidermal promiscuity, the confusion of bodies, lips, buttocks, hips – a single fractal entity disseminated beneath the membrane of the sun.

This human hyperorganism puts one in mind of that other huge organic individual in Canada – the world's largest – made up of 45,000 aspens, all sharing, through their mingled roots, in the same telluric life, the whole forest constituting a single vegetal entity. In the same way, all these Brazilian bodies make up a kind of single being, living the same life, with the same fluids coursing through them, aquiver with the same passions. What social or political status can there be for an entity of this order?

From the Montreal snowstorm to the Rio heatwave: the diagonal of the perfect journey. From underground complexes designed to last out through six months of winter to thoroughfares seething with naked bodies and an insane level of traffic. From respectful, moral comfort to warm, wild confusion. From consensual, air-conditioned space to sensual, tropical space. From human difference, made up of multiculturalism and tolerance, to animal intolerance, composed of unselfconsciousness and violence.

The only common factor between the northern and southern hemispheres is that generation you see everywhere, in all latitudes, running, jogging or walking, and high on phobic concern for their bodies. This is the New International Hygienic Order, the order of the repressed and the disembodied of modern society, of the disabled of the Virtual, who always seem to have just escaped from their wheelchairs and to be on the point of returning to them. This is the hygiene of the Assassins.

Telecom snobbery: getting yourself phoned up everywhere on your direct mobile line: in the street, on the underground, at friends'. An instrument worthy of the *Précieuses ridicules*, and quite the equal of the fans they carried. We have to do better, be more snobbish, even more convivial: from now on, rather than have my cleaning lady come to me, I'll go to her flat.

The charm of sleepless nights is the idea that tomorrow will not come. It is the idea of prolonging night and time as pure illusion, as in sleep and dreams, but without at the same time losing consciousness.

Ballard's *War Fever* provides the counterpoint to *La Guerre du Golfe n'aura pas lieu*. There, he has the Third World War taking place without anyone knowing it. Both are equally true.

In first-class air travel at night, you are already in 2001: the lines of cataleptic bodies leaning into the direction of flight (the lowest drag coefficient for entering death). Similar to space sarcophagi, whose vital functions are regulated by computer, or the *Énervés* of Jumièges,[13] or Hopper's recumbent figures, lying parallel in their deck chairs on their verandas, awaiting the end of the world and the end of the day.

The fate of the world's smart set on the first night of the century. New Year's Eve at Manaus. That famous night when the liner packed with the members of international 'high society', who had been invited to a party of unprecedented splendour by the rich city of Manaus in deepest Amazonia, drifted off into the night, carrying its passengers to their deaths in the meanders of the river, in the tortuous paths of the forest. One dreams of the amazing opportuneness of such a collective sacrifice today – of an end to the world elite in the year 2000 to echo that of Manaus in the year 1900. It is said that the Japanese are already secretly building a huge liner intended for this *de luxe* holocaust.

From the copro-paedophilic film to the Tibetan lecture, from the bio-aesthetic exhibition to the virtual images – what things we are expected to swallow in seven days! We have become real gullets. And not even time for proper deglutition. Fortunately, digestion and excretion are instantaneous. All ingestion of sounds or images, all information, has its built-in laxative, its innate obsolescence.

Her screen double does not look like her, but is tense, uncommunicative and graceless, in spite of her efforts to please. In real life, she does not have to make any effort. She is naturally vivacious, artful and affectionate, witty and scheming. She is still like that on the set, too, during filming. Now, on the screen, she is no longer that way at all. Did the lens capture someone else? Generally, the camera idealizes people and faces. Perhaps, in her case, she carries out this work of narcissistic idealization so well on herself every day that the camera can only disfigure her.

He does not define concepts, he does not analyse them, he does not criticize them: he murders them (but the crime is never perfect).

Just as blood is cleansed before being reinjected into the bloodstream, the real is whitewashed before being reinjected into the networks of the virtual.

The old haemophilia wounds keep on being infected. The hatreds, the defences, the debarments continue. People are hooked on their grievances as they are on a drug, hooked on the injection into their veins of a liquid that prevents the body from rotting. Animal spirits watch over a body in a state not of decomposition but of advanced preservation, immunized by archaic jealousy.

Being against war, telling stories, singing in the shower – these are the signs of a pleasant disposition.

Animals are under the illusion of the world and of their own lives. Even if they fight to survive, they have no knowledge of the reality principle. It is no doubt thanks to this reality stratagem that we have subjected, tamed or eliminated them. But this is nothing to be proud of.

In French, we say not the slightest *glimmer* [*lueur*] of intelligence, but not a *shadow* [*ombre*[14]] of proof. Not a *glimmer* of hope, but not the *shadow* of a chance. Shadow and glimmer are virtually interchangeable. And, indeed, why not switch them? A shadow of hope, a glimmer of despair?

The elixir of nullity
the mitigating circumstances
the gossamer difference
the clinamen of the will

The difference between ordinary silence and the silence of the desert, which has no equivalent anywhere else. A silence which always retains a certain animal, vegetal, atmospheric vibration – the trace of the vanished noise.

The contrast with the artificial silence of soundproofing, the silence of sensory deprivation tanks. Soundproofing is to natural silence what communication is to speech.

To secrete a protective conceptual illusion under cover of which one can slide peacefully towards one's homeostasis.

The modern ideal is to make your life what you want it to be. In reality, that is what you do when there's no other solution.

Sublimation: the direct transition from solid to gas. The ice vapours on the surface of the St Lawrence.

The man throws himself into the dustcart, shouting, 'I'm rubbish!'[15] They pull him out and he throws himself in again, shouting, 'I'm rubbish!' He had lost the use of metaphor.

The Mongols listening to the Gregorian chant in the gardens of the priory of Saint-Hymer. In fact, they are not listening to anything. They are waiting for the Mass to end, to see Baroness X go by in her wheelchair.

The 'private view' is the generic space–time of our cultural world, just as whitewashing is the black box of our political world.

I've nothing against concepts engendering other concepts. But only on condition that they lose their virginity, their legitimacy and their virtue. They have to obey only the system of thought which governs them, not their literal definition or their meaning. Humpty Dumpty: I make words mean what I want them to mean. I should like to see them disobey me.

To see – with a clear eye, an eye made perspicacious by death – the women in your life file past your glass coffin, first in chronological order, then in random sequence, then naked and as you knew them, in the first flush of youth and full of passion or regret. That, for a man, is the true synoptic résumé of his life, the erotic death throes, heightened by the sense that they might still, beneath the veil of their sadness, be jealous of each other. You can always dream.

At the heart of the Pyramids, there was a central space from which immortality radiated. At the heart of our civilization, there is now merely a hole into which the dustbins of history are emptied.

The human genome has its dustbins too: the 90 per cent of useless, 'selfish' genes. Might not nature, like our production system that has run wild, have just kept on producing genes which have – and can have – no purpose, except to pose an insoluble problem for the imagination?

It might seem that IT devices will provide future society with the incestuous base necessary for the solidity of any group or any couple. Each individual monad rigged out with its computer and copulating freely with it will be automatically preserved from any hint of eccentric passion.

That creamy, evanescent substance which, even unconsciously, keeps our bodies in a dreamlike, semi-hypnotic state, that shadowy side which protects us from total transparency and vigilance, that dreamy portion which sleeps within us even into our waking, active lives: a vital function, hounded today by the permanent demand for constant vigilance in the service of reality.

The imbroglio of safety and death. In Quebec, where the use of safety belts has considerably lowered the death rate from road accidents, there is a shortage of organs for transplant.

The two twins, one of whom is in prison.

At visiting time, the one takes the other's place. The prisoner is out, and the other twin merely has to have himself released on the grounds that he is there by illegal constraint. Ultimately, the switch doesn't even have to take place – as soon as the one twin is out, the other can always claim to be the innocent one. And if they are recaptured, which one will go back to prison?

In the same way as there are clandestine workers, so now there are clandestine non-workers (the clandestine unemployed). The black economy of non-work is competing with the black economy of work.

So far as Salman Rushdie is concerned, the Westerners have, in a sense, been carrying out the Iranian *fatwa*, substituting for violent death promotional sacrifice and dissolution into the sentimental world of the commodity in the legendary guise of the intellectual as victim. The Iranian strategy consists in infecting Western culture with fear, duplicity and self-pity.

Phobic aversion to that royal jelly of residual objects which live in the recesses of our existence and feed, like mites, off our desquamations. Warhol swept all this up at regular intervals, and packed it into cardboard boxes or packages which he stored away as archives.

Just as haemophiliacs are unable to staunch the flow of blood, so, semiophiliacs that we are, we are unable to staunch the flow of meaning.
Haemorrhage, Semorrhage
Haemophilia, Semophilia
Just as those receiving blood transfusions run the viral risk of AIDS, so those receiving language transfusions run the viral risk of the contamination of meaning.

That male beetle which dies without being born, since it is doomed solely to fertilize the other females in the womb which conceived them, after which it perishes without seeing the light of day.

Any personal contact becomes problematic – appointments, interviews, dinners, meetings. Relief of being shot of these things on any pretext whatsoever. The social game is made up of these distancing techniques.

In keeping with the unbreathable context of our culture, I have lost a third of my lung capacity. Is it better to breathe perfectly when the current atmosphere is unbreathable?

Moreover, if all breathing were to decrease by a third, the problem of carbon-gas pollution and the greenhouse effect would be solved.

In any event, we shall soon need gills to survive in this gaseous opacity and aquarium-like transparency. We shall have to become fish or aquatic reptiles.

The wave of cold which has just swept over North America does indeed seem to be criminal in origin.

The earthquake which has just struck the east coast of Japan could itself also be criminal in origin (that is what the people of Tokyo believed of the 1923 earthquake, and it is why they immediately massacred thousands of Koreans). Where do criminality, conspiracies and terrorism end? Where does the objective terrorism of natural forces begin?

Usefulness always has an object, by definition, whereas uselessness has none. Now, might it not be essential to know what a thing was useless for? What are the 90 per cent of non-specified genes useless for? What am I personally and specifically useless for?

Every effort to make me save time by using a computer is criminal. Making *me* save time – I who do not know what to do with it (this is perhaps what I am useful for: saving the species of the idle, which is under threat of extinction). In any event, time and space are naturally useless, and time saved is as serious as blood spilt.

In his film, C.M. has his childhood acted by his own son. Is it imaginable to have your old age acted by your own father? But you would have to take care not to have him act your own death.

There is only one way to finish, and that is to swallow your umbrella and thus, at the same time, the possibility of opening it: the image of death and rigor mortis.

But there are two ways to be free of your end again. Either not fully to use your capabilities (the man who doesn't open his umbrella even when it is raining) or to pass beyond your capabilities into an undefined field (for example, opening your umbrella even when it is not raining). The problem remains one of knowing whether you can pass beyond without going to the very end. In other words, whether you can become immortal without passing through death.

Now, beyond the end, we do not know what happens. The umbrella's enigma remains unsolved.

Without raising a stink,
Or even much of a laugh.

The zero degree of disorder and of events. The miraculous point of a total equilibrium. All affects arrayed neatly in the void of the soul. All functions arrayed neatly in the void of the body. Silence of the body and stillness of the world around you. You can dream of giving your life this profile and turning it into a sum of insignificant details. But some detail will always assume inordinate importance again, and wipe out all your efforts.

Socialism thought it had contracted a legitimate union with History. Without ever having courted it, it thought it was humanly possible to take history for its own. Hardly had it got into bed with it than it became the eternal cuckold. It must be said that history had whored around in lots of ways long before it met socialism, and all that remained was to enjoy the remnants of a corrupt history or the phantom of a vanished one. The last we heard, it had been kidnapped at this century's end, and no one is willing pay the ransom.

The French Socialist Party escaped a necessary, salutary dissolution – one which it surely has coming to it – by the symbolic suicide of one of its members, poor old Bérégovoy, who dissolved himself. But this sacrifice of a living being is of no avail, since the Socialist Party has long had its future signed away by a dead one – Mitterrand – who alone has absorbed all its substance.

The only act the PS could honourably have performed in recent times would have been self-dissolution. That sacrificial auto-da-fé, that active suicide of which it is quite incapable, was posthumously performed for it by Bérégovoy. It thus confirms the rout of the Left, but at the same time whitewashes it, and the Left will have no scruples about taking advantage of the situation. But the gift it has presented to the Left, and to the political class in general (politics is a noble calling because you can die for it), is a poisoned chalice, since it highlights the cowardice and wretchedness of all those who, faced with the same impotence and dishonour – that is to say, with the same reasons for ending their own lives – were very careful not to do so.

The exercise of power has always involved the risk of death: above and beyond the political, these are the rules of the symbolic. It is the price to be paid for public life not subsiding into total indifference. In this sense, B.'s suicide is the only political act we have seen in a very long time.

It seems likely, however, that the political class will not draw the only lesson worthy of it from that act – namely, that in certain extreme situations the only true act is that of suicide, dissolution or disappearance in one way or another – and that it will, rather, attempt to disqualify that death by beatifying it.

This death also casts light on the alleged legal offensive against corruption to which it secretly corresponds in the prospect it holds out of whitewashing the political class. The problem is this: the political class, and the Left in particular in recent times, is moping around in immunity and impunity. Moving in a weightless state, far, far from the social body, it is dying on the other side of representation, in the tele-absence of the masses, in what has become a lethal immunity with regard to the tele-citizen, who has himself become autoimmune. The absolute imperative is, then, to end that impunity by any means whatever, including its being accused of and exposed in scandals (very mildly, it must be said), to give it a chance to break out of its confinement and reconnect the umbilical cord. This is a question of life and death for the politicians. Now, they are quite incapable of renouncing their privileges of their own accord (they are capable only of granting themselves a collective amnesty). They therefore delegate the judges to do this work, as it were. They use the judiciary to absolve them of their immunity, to clear themselves of their corruption by presenting it dramatically, to free themselves of their confinement by appearing in the end vulnerable, fragile and, as a result, open and accessible.

It is a huge illusion to believe that in our system the political class and the judiciary can really come into conflict. This is merely a collusive division of labour within a caste, which is performing a simulacrum of a purge on itself – destabilizing itself in homeopathic doses the better to restabilize itself – without any great chances of long-term survival.

The two extremes; the aboriginal and the Western intersect here like nowhere else on earth, and squint at each other in a kind of anthropological strabismus. But, deep down, why try to wrench the aborigines out of the Stone Age? And why wrench ourselves out of our advanced technological state? It is as absurd as wrenching children from childhood or old people from old age. This we do everywhere by insinuation or electric shock on the dynamic path of our providential humanism.

If we could bear ourselves as we are, we could bear savages as they are: dishevelled, wild-eyed and staring – and ourselves, secretly corrupt and degenerate.

Cultures, taken in themselves, are not moving towards each other. Or, if they are, they are doing so as slowly as tectonic plates. The dream of reconciling them all one day is an absurdity. From the point of view of the universal, which is our point of view, they can only be exterminated – including our own. The space left for any culture by Western un-culture can only be that of *le mort* [the dead man, but also the 'dummy' at cards].

The hundreds of tourists massed on the site of Ayer's Rock waiting for sunset. The Tour Operators lay out the tablecloths, ice-buckets and champagne across from the sacred monolith. Irony of fate: that evening, there is no sun, no sunset. All the same, everyone carries on staring at the rock and filming it without let-up, but with no great hope either. The event is down on the programme and the tourists devour its absence the way TV viewers devour the empty screen on strike days. It has to be said that the genuinely anthropological spectacle of this urbane simulation in the middle of the desert was every bit the equal of a sunset.

By its geographical, geological and anthropological distance, Australia provides a total screen against the conventional stupidity of the state of the world. The hubbub of news becomes bewilderingly meaningless. Aboriginality (simply, originality?) is precisely this: a sidereal irony which screens out the irritation of business, the effusion of ideas and, above all, the incessant irradiation of current affairs – shadow of carcinogenic radiation as a result of the thinning of the ozone layer, which the Australians, precisely, complain of, and protect themselves from, with total sunblock. They also protect themselves from any intellectual radiation by an absolute pragmatism, turning their backs on the immense potential of aboriginal power which they possess and we no longer have.

During the thirty hours of the flight I contracted a time virus: the endless elongation of dead time. The plane seems to be standing still above the same deserts. No way of taking your mind off it. The countdown is there on the cabin screen: 'Distance to flight destination – 8,000 km.' Enough to drive the imagination to distraction. Even impatience and the passionate desire for the whole thing to be over end up wearing off.

On the ground this impression lasts for several days. Time is no longer flowing; it has become sticky. Ordinarily, every activity, whether of work or leisure, at least keeps the temporal flow going. Now, in this distracted state, you have the impression that the various activities are no longer eating up time. It is something like a breakdown of one's internal clock brought on by this overlong crossing of the world at altitude. It is as though time itself had suffered a prolonged oxygen deficiency.

Moving from winter to spring in January (Rome), then going back to a rainy winter (Paris), setting off again into subtropical summer (Caracas), and back again to early spring and a dull Paris. Then, suddenly, summer in Alice

Springs and, immediately after, autumn in Sydney and – at last genuine spring in Paris, in May. The jumble of seasons is one of the beauties of travel.

Treilles – the desert, the hermit's life – where the year converges to a blind focal point. The intellectual comedy goes on elsewhere. Here, it is a kind of rite – the ritual of the exorcism of all restrictions, all responsibility, all sociality, of the physical unpairing of thought and the body, confronted with the luminous distinction of the elements. Can something as conceptually desertic as the perfect crime match up to this mineral nature, this wind, this solitude? Last year, the double accident of being buried under the ashes and the wind scattering the texts had, as it were, put a temporary halt to the business. New stakes this year, double or quits.

Every year, I verify here, alongside the intelligence of the mineral world and the animal kingdom, the proportional stupidity of the human race – the deculturated peasants and acculturated tourists, arrogant adults and children with their pretentious technical gadgetry and senseless chatter. All the other species are more docile and spiritual in their silence than this one.

Why does the period before birth barely interest us, whereas the period after death excites us enormously? Most people anticipate it by arranging to live as though they are already dead. They anticipate their own disappearance by making themselves increasingly transparent, by making an inventory of the objects which will survive them. Not one of these must move. Everything must be in place for the final photograph.

People are obsessed with their posthumous tranquillity rather than with their happiness in this world to a degree that is quite insane. Deploying all their resources to wipe themselves out of their own lives right now. Setting up the backdrop to their absence in order to test out, while still alive, the fact of no longer being there. Carrying out all the daily tasks of a peaceful death. Doubtless, this is because they do not believe in immortality and hope only for a peaceful experience of death.

Get away from your life. Get away from your shadow on the wall.

Reading *Rabbit*, I fantasized about the clinical beauty of the 'percutaneous transluminal coronary angioplasty'.[16] A month later, a life-size coronary. You have to be careful what you read. And what if I hadn't read it?

In any event, the real episode is less poignant than in books. The real is always a bit laughable when it pretends to realize itself. That's not what was expected of it.

Cutting through the last umbilical cord that unites us to the real with your own teeth, while your nails dig into your memory in the absolute silence, and the flies endlessly violate our airspace.

It is not illusion which conceals reality. It is reality which conceals the fact that there is none.

The world must not assume the form of non-meaning and radical illusion. This latter must remain so well concealed beneath the obvious fact of reality that you pass by without noticing it.

In a book, too, there must be an idea so well concealed that you pass by without noticing it.

Adversity no longer exists within the subject, which has become indifferent to misfortune and to itself. Between the object and the subject of vengeance, no demarcation. A single, dual being, and nothing is separate.

The universe is mystagogic. It talks without knowing it, and without anything meaningful in its speech. Pedagogues speak in full knowledge of what they are saying, but they treat us like children.

The anatomists of the fifteenth century, suddenly discovering in the body, the nerves and the circulation of the blood a world of a radical objectivity, beyond God. Do we have anything equivalent today to such an upheaval, to such a displacement of all previously acknowledged facts? The discovery of the Unconscious was almost such an upheaval, but it no longer is. Doubtless, the exploration of the brain is the extreme adventure, which is likely to sweep away all our values and modern superstitions – *our* theology. But this is not necessarily progress. Just as the soul was swept away by anatomical dissection, so the body – and many other things too – will be swept away by the subtle dissection of the functions of the encephalon.

The persistence is great, but the difference is weak. And if the difference is weak, that is because the dehiscence is nil. And if the dehiscence is nil, that is because the effect is at a maximum, and the facts are recognized. And if the facts are recognized, that is because your sister's no better than she should be.

For every concept, you have to find the critical mass in order to arrive at a chain reaction in events and in heads. There is no real action without a prior chain reaction in ideas and in language, without a supercooling of the concept and language which cuts, at a stroke, through the geological strata of thought and action.

The friendly illusion of the coronary, of itself, ushers in a sabbatical year. Criminal perfection is linked to the Sabbath, the Coronary and the Heatwave.

The American miracle, even today, is that they have swallowed their own radiant, expansive image and spat it out in the form of dejecta, and that they continue blithely along their chosen path even if it is tending towards a catastrophically extreme situation. The miracle is that they have succeeded in collapsing fiction and reality into each other on a life-size scale, allowing themselves to be invaded by their own future (which is quite a different matter from living in real time); that they have managed to maintain a gravitation of centrifugal elements, of all these eccentric populations, minorities and exogenous cultures (paradoxically, they are today the country with the least risk of ethnic, linguistic and religious dislocation). Perhaps this is gravity's rainbow.

Rwanda. All the media say clearly where the killers and the instigators (and this includes us) are, and yet the whole business carries on. There is total information, but to no effect. Consensus and collective cowardice use this generalized state of informedness as their alibi. It functions as a scalpel, forever separating the juntas in power in every country in the world from any collective will, and, as it were, cauterizing all the contradictions which may ensue.

Can you, by setting the video recorder for the same time on the previous day, resuscitate yesterday's programme?

Can we, by reversing the digital clock at Beaubourg, turn the century around to run backwards? This would be the supreme terrorist act. But there is not even any need to perform it: the turnaround of history has already taken place.

History reproducing itself becomes farce. Farce reproducing itself becomes history.[17]

The objective is always to pull out the tablecloth without in any way changing the arrangement of the table.

You never have both the cards and the rules of the game at the same time.

In the empty space of desire, the seats are expensive.

The presupposed Adamic ipseity is priceless.

All terms with negative prefixes are already stereotyped language.

You don't get what you want just by wishing for it. And, indeed, you often don't get what you wanted precisely because you wished for it. Whereas if you don't know what you want, it doesn't hurt not to get it. And, at the same time, this solution preserves the possibility of getting something without having wished for it, which is the most charming hypothesis.

I slipped into this tricky business like a cat into a sack, and all the lubricious vipers began to writhe. I am referring to this unrealizable book which is wriggling around without me, and which I perpetually have to reimplant like an artificial embryo. It is the same with books now as it is with children – what's the point of bringing them into the world? It's enough just to think them up and carry them in your head.

These postmistresses, young and old, who have been given brand-new computers to sit at. This is to sit hot-blooded animals in front of cold-blooded technologies. What can come of it but a grotesque situation?

Benveniste: with the molecules rarefying to the point where they disappear completely, there remains the efficacy of the absent molecules, of the electromagnetic waves dissociated from their substance. This is perfect virtuality. No more substance in the molecular message – the medium alone produces the radiation. This is the ultimate stage of the transfiguration of the world into pure information.

It is hard to understand scientists' vehement opposition to this hypothesis, for this maximum abstraction, this virtualization of effects, is wholly in line with the most recent science. It is, therefore, morally and philosophically that the hypothesis is unacceptable. The possibility of effects without causes is deemed immoral. It is the breaking of the contract with the real, the philosophical denial of reality. Hence the anathema and the charge of heresy.

The world, for its part, has no need of real causes. Only the mind demands an explanation.

Having said this, what do you do with the 'real' molecule once its message can be passed on as electromagnetic waves? What do you do with Pavarotti once his voice has been synthesized? What do you do with the real once it has been rendered useless by the virtual? A Museum of the Real? A Conservation Institute? Should we store it up or conserve it as we do with endangered species? The absent real, effaced by its double, will be a potentially dangerous phantom. As with any waste product, there is a danger that we shall never be able to get rid of it.

Why are criminal acts and anomalies imputed to a chemical or bio- logical process, but never virtues and good deeds? It does indeed seem that only Evil has a right to an 'objective' explanation. Which suggests that scientific rationality might itself be merely a deeper form of this principle of Evil.

No difference between reality and the superstitious faith in reality. Preserving the real and preserving phenomena are leitmotivs of contemporary imbecility. Appearances, for their part, are always preserved.

The psychiatrists and analysts and all the psychological and social experts complain that they have to repair the immense damage done, to children in particular, by the social, parental and educational systems. But this human wastage is their stock in trade, whether they be therapists, politicians or social workers and the like. If everything only went well, the social welfare field would disappear, and all these fine people would be laid off. The system feeds, then, on its own misfortune. And every agonizing revision or alternative would involve an even more complicated, even more perverse machination.

Why not photograph human beings? Too sentimental. Even plants and animals are too sentimental. Culture is sentimental. Even historical violence is sentimental. Only objects, colours, light and substances have no sexual or sentimental aura. You do not have to violate them in cold blood to take their photograph. Not having passed through the mirror-stage, they are marvellously self-identical and have no problem of resemblance. By photographic technique, you can only add to the magical fact of their indifference, to the innocence of their staging, and thus bring out what is embodied in them: the objective illusion and subjective disillusion of the world.

Is there a politics of evil or ills [*le mal*] rather than of misfortune [*le malheur*]? We always act as though the victims (of AIDS, drugs, etc.) were somehow merged with their misfortunes, while yet being innocent of their own afflictions. We never credit them with responsibility for what afflicts them (including illness). We merely confront them with their misfortune and confine them to their promotion as victims. We even, through this official solidarity, undertake a kind of false advertising for them.

We never take into account what might be put down to connivance, to a provocation of the ill, if not indeed to choice and defiance, in this – unconscious or quasi-deliberate – acting-out in the fatal zone. It is the same with those who commit suicide; their act is always put down to depressive causes, no account being taken of the originality of the act itself.

We have to pity current medicine, which is as disarmed before ills [*le mal*] as priests are in their grapplings with the unconscious. This is because illnesses became interactive long before medicine came on the scene. They have been so for a long time, as have bodily functions: floating pathology, multiple interactions, wandering symptoms. And this is not even to mention the interactivity of infectious agents, of bacillae, microbes and viruses with vaccines and the various types of medication, which is easily on a par with the interaction between insects and insecticides: interactive response, reciprocal adaptation. Interactivity operates in every direction – for better and for worse. And to this we must add the interaction between the doctor and the patient, now supposed to have knowledge: another factor generating uncertainty in the division of responsibilities.

The masses now intervene directly in the spectacle, in the performance, in the event, by way of viewing figures, and through modems and the like. They have become interactive! In the opinion polls, we are all virtually present in the percentages: enforced interactivity. This desire for interaction in all fields is, at all events, quite pointless: we have long been interactive every-where, willy-nilly, through all the automatic response systems to which we are enslaved. And the dynamic interactivity which is everywhere held out to us as a source of artificial salvation will never be anything like as effective as the passive interactivity to which we are already subject – the interpassivity which interactivity merely extends with its techniques for producing voluntary involvement.

Interactivity is the end of spectacle. It all began with the abolition of the stage and the immersing of the spectator in the spectacle: Living Theatre. When everybody becomes an actor, there is no action any longer, there is no stage. Only with the strict separation of stage and auditorium is the audience fully an actor.

The revolution of 'lived experience' is without doubt the worst, the revolution which has swept away the secrecy with which everyone surrounded their own life and has transformed that life into a huge 'reality show'. What has been liberated by all the revolutions of desire, expression, fantasy and analysis is not the dramaturgy of the unconscious or the theatre of cruelty, but the theatre of banality. It is not the taboo on the drives that has been removed, but that on triviality, naivety, idiosyncrasy and idiosyncretism. What has been liberated is not each person's singularity, but their specific stupidity – that is to say, the stupidity they share with everyone else.

The specific idiocy of our time is, sadly, no longer differentiated from its intelligence. It is merged with it. It is no longer uneducated, but is indeed overinformed and has the same reflex vivacity as artificial intelligence. It is the degree Xerox of stupidity which merges with the degree Xerox of intelligence.

All in all, the soaring statistical rise of world stupidity – fifty million copies of the Pope's book sold in record time – is comforting, since you tell yourself that such a state of deliquescence cannot but produce a violent reaction, and that the world cannot end on such a pathetic statement of affairs – which leaves a degree of hope stored up against the future. But you may also entertain the opposite fear – that exponential stupidity will create a dizzying in-draught.

The deprogramming of language will be the work of language itself.
The deregulation of the system will be the work of the system itself.
The derealization of the world will be the work of the world itself.
Such is the prophetico-inert: prophecy fulfilling itself.

On closer examination, it was the very tenor of the revolutionary slogan: the workers will liberate themselves. Except that this contained a dangerous mystification: it merely opened on to the practico-inert, on to the liberation of work as an end in itself.

It is not the world as it should be which puts an end to the real world, but the world as it is.

The paralytic in his wheelchair embodies the virtual reality of movement.

Our closest ancestors, the apes, fell into disuse. Too close to us. Not different enough. The *ne plus ultra* is to go back to the inhuman genesis of man: bacterium or dinosaur. That's where you'll find an origin worthy of a species with an eye already on its future inhumanity, the inhumanity of clones.

Pruritus, itching, is what remains of an apelike activity. It is indeed because man has stopped scratching himself that he has moved on to other activities. On the other hand, this freedom has put an end to a certain conviviality which was that of apes: 'Scratch one another!' Today, everyone scratches alone, which is both one of the forms of the decay of the social sphere and one of the most impoverished forms of the appropriation of the body.

The body, as incapable of animal extraversion as it is of harmonious introversion, becomes eroticized in facial or gluteal rashes. It disfigures itself for want of otherness. Erythema takes the place of anathema, of which it is the epidermal version.

We learn that, at the moment of the catastrophe, Pompeii was peopled only by squatters and poor people, by old women and degenerates. Another fine dream gone! The thought that a natural catastrophe might just once have struck the rich first – or even rich and poor indiscriminately – is yet another we must relinquish. God never gets it wrong. Only the *Titanic* remains, but one day we shall learn that it was only carrying emigrants whose path to Eldorado was cut off by a providential iceberg.

Thelma and Louise: the only great film about perfectly free women. Not 'liberated' but free, their freedom consisting not in making demands, but in creating the space before them and taking themselves as their only yardstick. Naturally, this can end only in a magical disappearance into the void thus opened up, in an excessive (and ironic) passing beyond the horizon – without resistance, without a second chance, without regrets.

You should never let the slightest glimmer of hope show through. The slightest weakness is immediately exploited by the fanatics of optimism. You have only to allude to the stars whose light has not yet reached us for all repressed hope to flood into this gap opened up in the future: 'So you believe in that, after all? You admit that all is not lost?'

The 'therapeutic window'. What a delicious term for the interruption of medical treatment! Might you perhaps hurl yourself into the void through this therapeutic window? How about a hermeneutic window from which to hurl yourself beyond meaning? Or an existential window from which to hurl yourself out of existence and the perpetual reasons for existing?

Serendipity – a spectral term which denotes finding something one was not looking for, coming upon something unexpectedly. It is a name Christopher Columbus could have given to his caravel. But in fact, that discovery of America was not really a chance event. The Whites merely fulfilled the Indian prophecy which predicted the destruction of the race by beings from elsewhere. The Whites were merely the instrument of that prophecy by which the Indians met their end.

The strange assent among homosexuals to their being defined genetically. They prefer their difference to be biologically legalized. In the end, everyone prefers genes as the perfect alibi. The unconscious served in its time as universal justification. But that was still a psychical agency. Now it is biology that is becoming the juridical guarantee, the basis of legal argument. Difference, positive or negative, is being embodied in an immanent reason. Gene biology and sociobiology seem to have a bright future ahead of them.

In Amazonia, certain butterflies simulate the markings of their poisonous fellows to protect themselves. When you don't have the good fortune to be poisonous, you have to use deception. In this sense, we are all lepidoptera. Most of our behaviour is merely deception aimed at deflecting the great predator – death – from our path. Like the disguised lepidoptera, all our weapons are artificial ones – the innumerable strategies by which we shield ourselves from death and the inevitability of predation.

Moreover, what ultimately distinguishes the poisonous butterflies from the ones that adopt a poisonous appearance? What makes one species use a real weapon and another a simulated deterrent? And where we, the human race, are concerned, does all our armoury of machines, sciences and technologies function as a real weapon, or is it merely a gigantic simulation apparatus parading as real power?

Our consciousness being a kind of mirror, it follows that we appear to ourselves only symmetrically altered, like the image in a mirror. Everything which passes through consciousness must therefore be corrected and inverted for the true effigy (the essential, paradisiac form) to appear. This is part of the illusion of the world, whose trajectory can be corrected only by a supplementary artifice. We have to undo this with a mental turnabout, with the simulation of an inverted image – showing us as we shall never actually appear to ourselves.

Hence, the betrothed at a Pakistani wedding together enter a room in which there is a mirror. They look at each other only in the mirror. In this way, each sees the other as they are in paradise – that is to say, as they are really, in the transformed, essential image eternity provides of them, and not as they ordinarily appear.

No woman pre-empts a desire that has deliberately been restrained out of consideration for her. She is too happy to keep it in suspense – just as it is God's strategy, according to Gracián,[18] to keep man eternally in suspense. She savours the imagining of it for herself, at some length, but in so doing she increases the obsession in the one who desires her, to the point where she is possessed in the end only by a man obsessed with his own desire. Now, it is at this point that the woman becomes truly an object: when the only man who desires her is one preoccupied with his own desire. But in the end this suits everyone, since the woman, too, prefers to take her pleasure by interposition of an eternally unsatisfied desire.

That passionless, loveless woman who hires a recently jilted geisha to do her loving for her and to be sad in her stead. When her lover returns, the geisha rejects him, preferring to remain with the woman who has appropriated her suffering and laid claim to her. The heady lure of their complicity is stronger than her desire for love. Can you find someone to be happy and sad in your stead? You should at least find people to think in your stead, without the natural development of the thought thereby being altered. For there is nothing to prevent you from discovering the subtle void of thought behind that other person, just as, behind the other woman's mask, the woman found the subtle void of suffering.

The deepest wish is, indeed, to find someone to think, suffer and decide in your stead: 'If I have a book to have understanding in place of me, a spiritual adviser to have a conscience for me, a doctor to judge my diet for me, and so on, I need not make any efforts at all. I need not think, so long as I can pay; others will soon enough take the tiresome job over for me' (Kant).[19]

The only objection to the transference of will is that it can be as wearisome to find someone to think for you as to think for yourself, more tiring to find someone to will than to will for yourself. To find someone to write the book I want to write is, for example, almost insurmountably difficult. It does, however, happen that one comes upon a thought which precisely transcribes one's own. In that case, the pleasure is doubled by this external complicity. Originality is merely a minor, secondary bonus to the pleasure of thought.

Individuality, too, is a secondary aspect of the will and desire. The will is never mine; desire is never mine. For them to be will and desire, they have to circulate and be exchanged as symbolic material.

For want of this symbolic devolution, we operate a technical transfer of all these functions on to machines – a transference of the human on to the inhuman. Now, if some human being thinks for me, nothing is lost. He is not lost, neither am I. Whereas if a machine thinks in my stead, we are both lost.

In fact, this stage of the transference on to the machine is past. Today, it is machines which transfer their functions on to man. Man's fetishization of the machine has been succeeded by the fetishization of man by the machine.

Today, it is man who has become the object of the perverse desire of the machine, of its desire to function at all costs.

The machine is no longer an excrescence or a protruberance of man – it is man who is now merely the sex organ of the machine (Burroughs). And this is still quite a large claim, for what sex is the machine? Man has, rather, become the inflatable prosthesis of a sexless machine – the phantom limb of a useless function. The infinite degree, the degree zero, degree Xerox of the libido.

Among those devices whose virtual libido man stokes up, there is of course the computer, of which man is the unconscious masturbator and his brain a hyper-object of concupiscence, but there is also the spectacularized body of woman, become a bachelor machine, a promotional and pornographic hypostasis, of which man is merely the sexless operator, the slavish voyeur, the auto-decoder.

The lament of the automatic cash dispenser.

∞

Looking in the mirror, everyone adopts a flattering pose. In front of the cash dispenser screen, everyone takes on an air of death. Such is the terrible reflection of money on a face – or rather, the abstraction of money on the absence of face. The faces are those of hostages on television, which light up only when they are released.

∞

They either know or don't know they are being filmed. In a vague sort of a way, they behave as though they are. Their behaviour is furtive, puzzled, indifferent. They would rather not be there.

∞

This is not the reflection of gambling on faces racked by the possibility of a fortune. It is the anxious mask of voracious collusion, lit by the advance recognition of money. Never calm, never 'cool'. This explains why the card is often forgotten – unconsciously left in exchange.

∞

Cards, that virtual money, protect us from the vulgarity of cash. But money itself, that artifact of value, protects us from the vulgarity of the commodity. And the commodity, that artifact of desire, protects us from the vulgarity of human relations. In this way, we are marvellously protected.

∞

The pure form of *jouissance* is value
The pure form of value is money

The pure form of money is banking
The pure form of *jouissance* is remorse.

∞

Can we imagine a video dispenser which would identify everyone by their smile, and not by their code or their fingerprints?

∞

The only possibility of play, the only real pleasure: fraudulent use of the card, the stolen card, duping the automatic universe, hoisting the machine with its own petard. Secret rejoicing, panic flush at the undiscovered crime.
The way that woman's face lights up after the successful fraud.

∞

Automatically dispensed money always produces the magic illusion of cargo cults: you win every time. As in the story of the Coca-Cola machine, in which someone puts a coin in and a can comes out. Another coin, another can. Third coin, third Coke. Mutterings in the queue: 'Let someone else have a go!' His response: 'Let me carry on. Can't you see I'm winning? So long as I'm winning, I'm going to carry on!'

We are threatened not just by memory loss, but by the routing of the synapses by the filterable viruses of memory. The strange disappearance of names, faces and places seems like a programmed erasure, like the imperceptible advance of a virus which, after infecting the artificial memories of computers, is now attacking natural memories. Might there not be a conspiracy of software?

After the age of pleasure and its libertine discipline came the age of desire and its sacrificial obligation. After the rule of pleasure, the law of desire. The two separated by many a revolution and liberation, including sexual liberation.

Today, both have aged a lot. Even desire has gone out of fashion. It is law which is the order of the day.

After pleasure, desire.

After desire, law.

And after law? There is no longer any telling. We imagined that law (like the State) was doomed to disappear in the interactivity of exchange, in the flow of communication. But, quite the contrary, it, like the State, is being reinforced – the two culminating in the new divinity of the *Rechtstaat*.

It is being reinforced by the loss of freedom, of our natural physical environment and all of what, up to now, was graciously given to us, without our having a right to it: such as life, for example.

Is it not the 'role of intellectuals' to concentrate the accursed share of thought on themselves, and thus purge the whole of society of it, which then becomes the freer to balance out good and evil for itself? Is it not their role to focus the sickness of thought on themselves, and to find a baleful use for it? As it is the role of politicians to focus the chronic sickness of the social sphere on themselves, which is the essence of power, and to find a political use for it. The arbitrary power of the ruler derives from the fact that he condenses in himself all the scattered, diffuse, arbitrary power within a society, to the point where that society is delivered of it. If arbitrary power is not concentrated at the summit, it is everywhere in society: so it is with the democratic state, where arbitrary power is diffuse and endemic, like the perverse effects of the structures of empire when they break up. Now, neither intellectuals nor politicians play this role any more. They aspire only to expressing, representing, guiding, rationalizing and enlightening. They rig themselves out with moral consciences, with suffering and witness, devotion and therapeutic zeal towards sick values (in which, naturally, they have a part). Worse, they seek to efface themselves so that everyone can express themselves – this is the senile disorder of democracy, piously discarding speech and power and handing them over to everyone. Of course, this hypocritical and apostolic auto-da-fé does not solve things, and they all end up dying all the same, though in a role which is not their own. As for society and thought, they are thus given over to confusion and internal virulence – literally to the transparency of evil, which no longer finds anywhere to manifest itself.

These toadying intellectual curs, always wondering how it is possible to be both a genius and politically despicable (Céline, Leni Riefenstahl . . .), it being understood that the essential thing is not to be a genius, but one of the right-thinking. Admittedly, most of them had no choice.

Philistinism and Pharisaism mingled, the arrogance of the good cause laying hold of radical thought – of the accursed share, of the philosophical interrogations of Artaud, Bataille, Debord and Nietzsche – to embody the integrism of legitimate thought in all their ardent masochism. For there is a strange consumption here of basic human suffering and the international defence of Human Rights. There is even a furtive revisiting of Marx, on tiptoe, in the hope that the Stalinist, episcopal blessing will rain down.

This is the New Intellectual Order.

Virtuous thought everywhere. Further and further from the thinking of Evil, from illusion, from ironic thought. A thought which has denied terror in all its forms (a denial brilliantly staged in the commemoration of 1789) except the form of gentle, inexorable terror it wreaks on itself and which might be termed the subjective integrism of our Western intellectual society – the orthodoxy of dissidence, as Zinoviev would say. More and more democratic, liberal, pluralistic, exchangist, 'cultural', fuliginous, altruistic, differentialist and referentialist, clerical, moral and convivial. Humanitarian. History has become a blow-up doll and humanitarianism is its condom. Humanitarianism is to thought what the blow-up doll is to desire. Thus, every problem has its inflatable solution, made up of the historical failure of desire.

All the ills of the political class, which is today falsely intellectualized, have in their turn infected the intellectuals. The cynical discourse of the politicians, the soft fundamentalism and integrism which characterize them, are desperately idealized by thoroughly contrite intellectuals with thoroughly bad consciences. 'We have only one culture, and we have to save it.'

At least humanism was linked to humankind, a rising political and cultural concept. Humanitarianism, for its part, is fundamentally linked to the human species, a declining biological and sociological essence. What is in play here is the whole difference of tone between a political and philosophical utopia for mankind and the management of the human species as a virtual waste product.

The Human shows through in a moving and mysterious way only in those who are bereft of it. Perhaps it has real presence only in animals, as we see in Canetti's work.

The idea of the Human can come only from elsewhere, not from itself – the inhuman is the only evidence for it. When it attempts to define itself – precisely by excluding the inhuman – it becomes laughable. When it seeks to realize its own concept – in humanism and humanitarianism, for example – it immediately passes beyond itself into violence and absurdity. Thought lives only at the outermost reaches of the human, at the asymptotic limit of the inhuman. If, as Canetti writes, the very idea of metamorphosis disappears from the universe when animals do, then there is neither man nor thought any longer.

Stigmatizing the millions of Italians as 'consenting victims' of Berlusconi, denouncing the stupidity of the masses and wrapping oneself in the flag of the divine Left and its democratic arrogance – this is the pose of the enlightened intellectual, who is prepared to leave his country as a punishment (though he does not do so).

All this comes from a short-sighted, conventional analysis of political Reason. The 'blind' masses, for their part, have a more subtle – perhaps transpolitical(?) – vision, to the effect that the locus of power is empty, corrupt and hopeless and that, logically, one has to fill it with a man who has the same profile – an empty, comical, histrionic, phoney individual who embodies the situation ideally: Berlusconi.

For abject power, an abject individual. Anything is permissible to shatter the illusion of the political, and to make this abjection shine forth to the world.

Who was it who talked of putting the imagination in power? The political world as it is corresponds exactly to the only possible 'reality'. Berlusconi is what he is, and all recrimination is simply the product of a shattered illusion.

But it is just as undeniable that we cannot bear either Berlusconi or the current state of affairs. We have, therefore, to take into account both the obvious fact that we have the system we deserve and the equally non-negligible fact that we cannot bear it.

The Whites are going to end up pulling out of Africa altogether, leaving the natives to their primal scene, the simian condition, condemned as they are to endemic AIDS and mutual extermination, thanks to the weapons we generously continue to send them. A whole continent is being sealed off – not to make it, as in the case of the Tasaday,[20] a protected sanctuary, but a sink to be done away with.

In the hold one exerts over others, suffering plays a great role. It is enough simply to suffer first to assume an advantage. Even in the exchange of suffering, what counts is having the initiative. In days gone by, you had to be quicker on the draw than your shadow. Today, you have to be quicker to suffer than your shadow. To jettison, to let go, more quickly than the other. Perhaps, too, to love more quickly than the other, to love before you are loved. For if no one shoots first any longer today, no one dares love first either.

Using virtue to immoral ends is banal. Using vice to restore one's virtue is a more original move. This is currently a fashionable political tactic. Protesting one's errors, one's corruption, one's immorality and scandals to get oneself denounced, accused, charged and condemned (even rightly condemned) is a form of simulated expiation among all the villains, an art of self-whitewashing in which the public conscience wallows at little cost to itself.

Amsterdam. The Boeing crashes on take-off, seemingly by chance, coming down on buildings occupied by illegal workers who are black immigrants from the Antilles. The thought of it – dying in a hell of aviation fuel! So unknown to the authorities were these illegal workers that not even their charred bodies have been found. Yet they were not sufficiently clandestine to prevent the hand of God coming along to strike them down in their clandestinity. This is all perfectly logical. And when we are dealing with a human, racist logic, we can understand why it should always be the same ones who are the victims. But when it is the inhuman itself, when it is objective fate and the random mechanics of a crashing Boeing (that is to say, God) which strike along these same lines, then this non-human racist logic poses a real problem for the metaphysical consciousness. No argument can equal the excessiveness, the outrageous injustice, the racial prejudice which bring it down on – of all people – these wretched immigrants with no social identity. In explanation, we can only suggest a higher ironic power, a providence of Evil playing cynically with extreme phenomena. This excess of injustice and transcendental discrimination in a way prove the existence of God, but they do so *a contrario*, by identifying him totally with the power of Evil.

Regarding the fidelity of a woman you love and who loves you, no cause for worry. For either she is unreservedly faithful to you – or she is cheating on you. And in the latter case, given all you know of her – or think you know – it would be such an incredible betrayal, such a spiritual disillusionment, that it would be a real negative proof of the existence of God!

And then, what revenge! What delight. The triumphal certainty of the principle of Evil! Is this not what we are passionately seeking? For want of proofs of God's existence, at least a radical proof of his nonexistence – for either Evil has no existence of its own, and functions merely by reference to the existence of Good, or there is an autonomous principle of Evil, and in that case the evidence of Evil is at least as reassuring to the mind as the evidence of God.

The joy of evil is not so much in doing it (do you ever know where it lies?) as in noting that a particular person in whom you have the most total confidence turns out to show the most total bad faith: that God himself – or chance, or a woman – can be so perfidious that this takes on the dimensions of a revelation. And that revelation has such force and engenders such stupefaction that any personal sadness, any moral disappointment, is swept away by the metaphysical manifestness of that immorality. The ecstatic form of disillusionment.

In the past, it was more in the abundance of Good that proofs of the existence of God were sought. Today, we have to fall back on the same proposition ironized and inverted. We have to look to the total disillusionment of the world, to the excess of the negative and of hardship, for the sarcastic proof of God's existence. The certainty which results is as comforting as, and more stable than, the other kind.

Yet let us be careful here: Evil itself has an unfortunate tendency towards dialectical recuperation. It has to be protected from this, and we have to beware of all reconciliation, for then, in the interaction of Good and Evil, all final certainty as to things being as bad as they possibly can be gets away from us and, consequently, all metaphysical exhilaration.

The dialectic of the emotions is like that of the sign and the ascendant. The two may be in conjunction or opposed. The sign alone is not enough: you have to have the ascendant too. It is not enough just to be happy: this has to give you pleasure too. It is not enough just to be unhappy: this has to hurt. Without the aura of pleasure, happiness is sad indeed; without the idea of pleasure, there is mere mammalian enjoyment. But without the aura of suffering, unhappiness is also sad indeed.

There is always a transcendence of pleasure or unpleasure beyond the fact of being happy or unhappy.

The hypocritical accounts which set happiness and unhappiness in opposition miss this subtlety which unites them in a common division – in that reversibility of each which, in the end, constitutes our true happiness. We still have the freedom to use this and to abuse it extravagantly, and only what takes this freedom from us makes us truly unhappy beings.

Can genetic theory be extended to the events of our lives and, more particularly, to the baneful micro-events with which they are peppered? Just as germs, bacillae and viruses are potentially present in each individual organism and rouse themselves at the slightest weakening or loss of immunity, so accidents, slips and baneful little events are aroused at the slightest mental weakening. You have the impression that they jump at the chance, that they take advantage of the slightest favourable moment to occur, to produce themselves.

Might not a certain kind of 'historical' event, relating in this case to entire groups of people – such as the resurgence of ethnic, linguistic and national 'impulses' – arise out of this kind of genetic reactivation in a phase when history is weakening and the social and political spheres are immunodeficient?

A huge proportion of the grey matter is mobilized by the banal functions of the living organism. Ninety-nine per cent of the physical, motor, memory and linguistic potentialities – and also of their potential for emotion, deception, play and seduction – is common to all the human beings in a society. This means that intelligence is merely a superficial phenomenon, and between the gifted child from a good family and the concierge's axolotl baby there is merely a tiny difference in the wiring of the neurons. Moreover, if only a small percentage of genes separates man from the ape, what separates an 'intelligent' human being from a 'stupid' one must be something even smaller.

But this does not diminish the moral and anthropological scandal of the uselessness of such a welter of neurons, of such a marvellous biological machine, compared with the foetal use the human species generally makes of it.

On some works of art, and not the most minor ones: they have all the appearance of worthlessness; they say they are worthless, and they truly are.

This is where the whole ambiguity of contemporary art resides: laying claim to worthlessness, insignificance, non-meaning and banality; straining for worthlessness, when it is in fact already worthless. Aiming for non-meaning when it is in fact already insignificant. Aspiring to superficiality in superficial terms. Minimal thought had already met the same unfortunate fate.

Everywhere the same incantation: I'm worthless, I'm worthless! Now, worthlessness is a secret quality which cannot be claimed by just anyone. Insignificance is the secret quality of a few rare works, works which never lay claim to it. The claim of worthlessness is, for its part, merely bluff and blackmail, aimed at extorting credit and a sense of importance *a contrario*, the implication being that the work cannot possibly be so worthless, that there must be something hidden in it. Contemporary art plays on this uncertainty, banking on the guilt of those who understand nothing of it (that is to say, those who have a precise intuition of what there is to be understood). I brought just one ill-defined impression back with me from Venice: that modern art is a conspiracy.

The paradox of abstraction, and hence of the avant-garde of modern art, is that, in believing it is 'liberating' the object from the constraints of figuration to return it to the pure play of form, it has tied it to the idea of a hidden structure, of a more rigorous, more radical objectivity than that of resemblance. In ultra-rationalistic vein, it has sought to push aside the mask of resemblance to get at the analytic truth of the object.

Bringing out this analytic truth of the object, the world and the social sphere by deconstructing their appearances is the aesthetic and political move of modernity. Now, it is precisely the opposite which needs to be done: one has to see through the identity to bring forth the mask. One has to see through the truth to bring forth the illusion and the secret alterity.

The more subtle approach is that which takes reality for a mask, resemblance for a trap, and plays on illusion through this very resemblance by making it more detailed, more obvious – too lifelike to be true. This is the secret of *trompe-l'œil* and, more generally, of a figurative art beyond representation, and beyond its illusory transcendence in the abstraction in which modern art is exhausting itself.

Objects and images are traps which reality is kind enough to walk into, playing an intelligent extra's role, but the traps never close on it, nor it on them. If illusions are always illusions of a reality, reality, for its part, is never the reality of anything but an illusion. Or rather, illusion does not stand opposed to reality, whether we are speaking of the illusions of childhood, war or love: it is a more subtle reality, which envelops primary reality in the sign of its disappearance.

Everything takes place as though in an empty room, which is the primal scene of absence, that scene where one is present at one's own absence and there is, therefore, no danger of getting lost.

This is how illusion operates: it restores to us beings and objects in the form they intrinsically take when changed by their absence, their disappearance. Vanished, but transparent to their own disappearance, whether this ensues from their origin or their end. It is in this sense that they deceive us, but are faithful to themselves. And this is why you have to be faithful to them, for it is in their detail, in their minute detail, in their exact figuration, that objects are illusory, that reality is illusory. It is in their exact linkage that objects constitute an event, because it is in the exactness of the world that true abstraction resides.

The whole world is merely an illusion of the senses and the sensory trace of that disappearance. It is in this sense that objects deceive us by the space, the distance from their own sources – but in the end, we become the object of the objects which deceive us, and we fall under the spell of that distance.

This distance is as much that from those stars which are dead, but whose light still reaches us, as from those which have been shining now for a long time, but whose light has not yet reached us.

This is to say that there is still hope.

The cinema today: end or impossibility of ending? Most current films, through the bloody drift of their content, the weakness of their plots and their technological trumpery – useless high-tech – reveal an extraordinary contempt on the part of film-makers for the tools of their own trade, for their own profession: a supreme contempt for the image itself, which is prostituted to any special effect whatsoever; and, consequently, contempt for the viewer, who is called upon to figure as impotent voyeur of this prostitution of images, of this promiscuity of all forms beneath the alibi of violence. There is in fact no real violence in this, nothing of a theatre of cruelty, but merely a second-level irony, the knowing wink of quotation, which no longer has anything to do with cinematic culture, but derives from the resentment that culture feels towards itself, that culture which precisely cannot manage to come to an end and is becoming infinitely debased – a debasement being raised to the power of an aesthetic and spiritual commodity, bitter and obsolescent, which we consume as a 'work of art' with the same complicity with which we savour the debasement of the political class. The sabotaging of the image by the image professionals is akin to the sabotaging of the political by the politicians themselves.

Thought makes cynical and immoral use of meaning, truth, reference and reality. The least formula is used by it to concept-corrupting ends. It prostitutes the idea in language, rather than prostitute language to the idea in the guise of 'ideology'. Rather than make radical use of authentic thoughts, it makes superficial use of thoughts from elsewhere, out of a relaxed attitude towards itself (Warhol: 'If I was sure everything came from elsewhere . . .').

It is not a question of conferring some kind of positivity on thought, since its operation is precisely to detract from the truth and the legitimacy of existence. And radicality doubtless has no other function than to provide an added bonus of pleasure.

A theory closed towards the outside but open on the inside. With no comment, no perspective and no outcome – what gets in does not come out again (for this same reason, it is very difficult to get in). It no longer produces information in the proper sense of the word – it is a poetic form of the disillusioning of meaning. Somewhat as there is an absolute event horizon in physics, there is here the absolute concept horizon. Nothing in this theory provides an answer to conventional questions, current or philosophical. Such answers as there are open on to another space: that of singularity and perpetual motion on an inner orbit, the effect produced in this world being solitude.

The book is there, entire in his head. Neither it nor its shadow has any rival in mental space any longer. It reigns there alone, by force of emptiness. But does anything remain to be said at this point? One has to face the fact: illusion is an insoluble material, an impossible concept.

Doubtless the final state of thought is disorder, rambling, the fragment and extravagance. What is the point, then, in putting order into a book? Why sustain this will, this design, which we see merely as a servitude to ourselves? However, it has to be written, because writing – unlike oral discourse, which, being destined to be heard, is made to come to terms with the order of things

– is the site of their fragmentation, their anti-gravity: it is where they are restored, by force of language, to an extreme singularity.

It has to be written, if only to lock away the real key to the story in a single page, and remove that page once the book is finished, so that no one will know what it is all about – as ever, the perfect crime. However, it must be possible for that page to be reconstituted without its secret being revealed, and this dispersal is the very mainspring of theoretical fiction.

Being a twin: the supreme curse.

To feel too much by half or only the half of oneself is the destiny of those twin sisters (the Gibbons sisters) who, in looking so much like each other, look like nothing on earth. The same gestures, same reflexes, same body, same speech. Their fusional huddling-up when they are in company is transformed, when they are alone, into verbal frenzy, sexual violence, the desire to kill or commit suicide (which, for them, amounts to the same thing). They end up taking their unbearable osmosis off into a psychiatric institution. But there is also twinship in that stammering man whose twin, whom he has never managed to slough off, stammers through him.

This is doubtless the true Oedipal problem for everyone. Not so much to free yourself from the parental triangle as from your virtual double, from that umbilical *alter ego* who, for each individual, is like a congenital figure of death. It is doubtless with this hidden twin, this virtual twin whom we all carry within us at birth, that we have the greatest difficulty breaking.

In *Dead Ringers*, the woman, in her dreams, tries to devour the umbilical cord to free the one she loves from this monstrous twinship. In fact, she is trying to give birth to him a second time. But she does not succeed. He will prefer twinship to sexuality, and twinned death to women and seduction.

I always arrive on time, even without trying. There is a kind of fatality about this, based on an unfailing internal accounting system. Day and night, even when I am awakened unexpectedly, I always know what time it is. Obsessional? Of course. But in our culture it is time itself that is neurotic. From the moment when 'two o'clock *means* two o'clock', there is no longer any normal solution to the problem of time. Whether you arrive on time, early or late, nothing is psychologically normal any longer. There is no longer any possibility of a free relation to time, except when it merges with space and speed.

Things which have remained hidden since the end of the world (but were not necessarily hidden at the beginning).

Events which pass by in the sky like unidentified flying objects.

'You must not believe that truth remains truth when you take its veil away.' So, truth has no naked existence.
You must not believe that the real remains the real after you have dispelled the illusion of the real. So, the real has no objective truth.

When you take away verisimilitude, you do not automatically find the veridical but, perhaps, the implausible.

Ideological language [*la langue de bois*] is a spongy language which absorbs the fluid secretions of thought the way a Tampax absorbs menstrual blood.

The hegemony of the nervous system will inevitably be succeeded by that of a hypernervous – nervy – system.

Telethon – AIDSathon – Thanaton – Marathon – all satellites of Benetton, which has indeed annexed them for its advertising.

With acceleration, the entire system is becoming centrifugal. There is, then, no virtue in eccentricity. But this centrifugence is at the same time creating a still, central zone, an eye where gravity is zero which, in a sense, preserves the reverse memory of the peripheral particles. In this blind zone, the laws are reversed. Everything makes sense in the reverse.

Man is an exaggerated being, and he brings a pathetic exaggeration to the world. Just what objective suffering results from this ought to be assessed – the pain of those things which suffer, if not from existing, then certainly at least from the fact that we exist. This is why Stoic teaching culminates not so much in the avoidance of human suffering as of the suffering inflicted on the world by our exaggerated and superfluous presence.

The secret services are as hidden as can be. Advertising is as visible as can be. What they have in common is that no one has ever been able to show that either has any effect whatsoever.

The Bride stripped bare by her bachelors, even – prophetic title. In the mechanics of the transpolitical, the transsexual and the transaesthetic, all desiring machines are becoming bachelor machines . . .

On every long-haul trip, the ozone layer protecting the memory begins to fray, the way the one in the stratosphere is fraying beneath the onslaught of spray cans and bovine flatulence. The hole through which memories escape into space is growing larger, prefiguring the great migration of the void to the periphery – of the void which every atom of our life contains near the outer reaches of death.

Whitewashing is the primordial activity of the current *fin-de-siècle* – the whitewashing of a dirty history, of dirty money, of corrupted minds, of the continents and the polluted seas. The whiteness of the Whites themselves seems merely that of racial purification.

From now on, everything goes directly into the heritage, without even passing through a real-life event. Events pass into history without even having taken place. Art goes directly into the galleries without having undergone the fate of an art work. Everything is produced as a fossil from the outset without having passed through the geological strata of time.

Foresight being the memory of the future, when everything is seeable nothing is any longer foreseeable.

We are today celebrating the twentieth birthday of 'Lucy', for naturally her real birth dates from her exhumation as a fossil, from her palaeontological resurrection. As a consequence, Coppens became her 'father'. His one-hundred-and-fifty-thousandth ancestor (in terms of generations) has become his offspring. Not everyone is presented with the chance of such a fine career by his own daughter.

We might wonder whether, in these necrolithic copulations, and with a goodly number of events that seem too good to be true, we are not each time being used to 'father' some dubious progeny.

The height of sexism is to regard the other sex as a different race. This is the objective of 'hard' feminism: a world expurgated of the male race. This is the same, though opposite, as happens in *Il mondo senza donne*.[21] The same eradication of the other on a homosexual basis, or a sisterly basis, a basis of twinship or incest.

The other tendency is, rather, to supplant men in positions of power. The male pole position being virtually unoccupied (since man has virtually disappeared), the feminists are in an enormous hurry to move into it, and they naturally fall into the trap that is the void of power itself. In the same way, political power being emptied of its substance, the Left rushed to seize it and immediately disintegrated in the void.

Two kinds of science fiction. The one fantastical and fabulous, playing on other worlds; the other paroxystic, extrapolating a detail, a characteristic feature and, by a rigorous logic, revealing its eccentricity or its extreme effects. Ballard's *Wind from Nowhere* and *Crash*, Zamyatin, etc., are examples of the latter type.

The subtraction of any single element can also serve as a stimulus for fiction – as, for example, does the total elimination of the female sex in *Il mondo senza donne*. But one can also imagine a world without men, without animals, without clouds, without images, without dreams: each hypothesis can produce a wonderful fictional story. We might think of Georges Perec's *La Disparition* or Chamisso's *Peter Schlemihl*, the man who lost his shadow. We might imagine, also, a world without reality, without a reality principle – it would have nothing but virtual extremities, phantom extremities (or limbs). This is, to some degree, the theme of *The Perfect Crime*.

The whole art is to substitute for our culture of bilateral blackmail – and of the insoluble dilemma of the double bind – a strategy of the double un-bind in which, instead of losing either way, you win in each case. Children know very well how to use a double strategy which comes out to their advantage whatever the demand made upon them: ironic consent, simulated denial, useless lying, superfluous dejection – in the end, it is the parents who are caught in the double bind.

The whole art of theory is, on this same model, to present two hypotheses which are equally true while also being contradictory: a paradoxical state which is also a felicitous one – a state of automatic resolution and immanent justice by the revenge of the world on the idea.

Even in public, women must preserve an aura of intimacy and inwardness. Hence this fashion among young women of walking in the street with their arms folded across their chests, as though they had just taken communion; or even with their arms crossed from shoulder to shoulder, as though embracing themselves. What would you say about a man who walked down the street with his arms folded?

Dinner at the consulate with various dignitaries present: what is known as a *dîner de têtes*. Not one woman there. You'd think you were at a gathering of the Mafia or the Freemasons. But no doubt a *dîner de têtes sans* women is better than a dinner with women *sans têtes*.

Three elements which balance out: a rural unconscious, an urban subconscious and a cosmopolitan consciousness.

Impatience is a millenarian passion which desires the immediacy of the end. Now today, wherever time has been abolished by the operation of 'real time', events no longer come to maturity, either immediately or with a delay. But impatience is not consoled by that: having nothing left to devour, it devours what remains of the real.

There is nothing left to protect us from the scene of the real. Nothing left to protect us from the obscenity of the virtual (of information, transparency, etc.). We are no longer the actors of the real but the double agents of the virtual.

Facts do not have to be true. Whether the world is a particular way or not, whether it has or has not fallen prey to simulation, changes nothing of the analysis. The 'real' fact is essential to the theoretical imagination – after that it has no importance. In any case, truth can come into being only in a theoretical space, and there is no theoretical space where verification is possible.

Necessity being the basis for order and morality, immorality always resides in anticipating the realm beyond necessity, in confusing the ideal and reality, or the system, with its own ideal (hence the parade in Red Square: 'We are all happy in the Soviet Union!') and acting, through excess, expenditure, prodigality and transgression, as though there were too much for everyone. However, this configuration is now behind us, because there is already too much today. Excess forbids us any subjective immorality. What prevails today is objective immorality, the immorality of systems which lack nothing and against which we can do nothing: their immorality is much more radical than ours. At the end of an all-too-human evolution, we join up again with nature and animality which are, for their part, objectively immoral, since they lack nothing.

For some people, ideas are exhausted in their reference, their history, their genealogy and their textuality – as are concepts in their literality and their etymological genesis. Now, ideas are phenomena like any others, and the laws of phenomena apply just as much to them. Just as we have to take phenomena without any preconceived ideas, so we have to take ideas without any preconceived reality – neither the reality which precedes them, nor that which follows them.

I nearly gave a lecture in India on the end of the Millennium, forgetting that the Indians do not have the same linear style of counting at all, nor the same conception of time. Basically, though, how do they manage (for they, too, also live in world time)? Is there not a rate of exchange between the one temporality and the other, as there is between foreign currencies, and are there not all kinds of speculation possible between the two?

I go to London for the presentation of the English translation of *Symbolic Exchange and Death*. I have an attack of renal colic (stomach pains). Now, I remember my last attack was fifteen years ago and that it occurred in Tübingen, where I had gone for the presentation of the German translation of *Symbolic Exchange and Death*. An extraordinary coincidence with no possible interpretation (no point going into an analysis of this). And there is, in the end, a certain joy in these unexpected spawnings of the body, which we believe we use as we wish but which, in reality, does as it pleases.

I have no courage and bear no grudges. I am therefore without character. If I had either of these characteristics, I would have reacted violently to a thousand useless things. It is, therefore, a form of philosophy.

I quite like wasting my time, but not having it wasted. When I am faced with too much calculated slowness, entirely affected even if circumstances impose it, or with the boredom exuded by certain of our contemporaries like a timeless virus, my impatience is unleashed – the only thing gained in the end being a bad conscience.

Servility is the fuel of power, and arrogance is its lubricant.

Eating tepid oysters and caviar with a KGB mole in a London restaurant.

The gift is impossible, he says. One never gives something up without taking something in return. But who said the gift was free – except in Christian idealism or economic theory? This critique is itself related to an idealist conception of the gift, which is the conception of a culture of equivalence and calculation. In a more radical anthropology, the gift is something quite different. It is a dual, antagonistic relation – a singular form, without equivalence. In this radical form, which still today governs if not our exchanges, then at least our ambivalent passions, it is not the gift but exchange that is impossible. The gift, for its part, is not only possible but inevitable [*fatal*]. It is the very form of impossible exchange.

If unilateral giving is impossible, the problem of the unilateral possibility of receiving none the less remains entire (a paradox analogous to that in which only one term differs from the other, the other not differing from that first term).

Are there not human beings capable of receiving with impunity, without giving anything in return, being themselves in a sense the immediate, living return for the gift? Beings so self-sufficient that they need to give nothing, to render nothing in exchange. But responding to the obscure desire we doubtless have for an ideal being who has no need of us. One may become attached to someone simply for the fact that he gives you nothing, offers you nothing – except the fact of existing, which is already quite something. A pure being, without reciprocity. An attractant without any opposite pole. Is this possible, and is there not in this a kind of human sacrifice?

If truth and reality can clearly come only from the subject and his consciousness, then illusion, which is the opposite of these, must necessarily come from elsewhere. From the world of the object, from some other thing than the subject. Illusion, like profusion, comes to us from the world.

Against the theological definition of Evil inherited by all the modern ideologies which shut Evil up in an idealist vicious circle, we must defend a Manichaean, antagonistic form of Evil, a form of genius, of originality of Evil and of irreconcilable heresy. Or, alternatively, a form of the reversibility of each, according to a Moebian topology which may actually be an even more radical heresy.

Hysteresia.
Those who continue to vote although there are no more candidates.
Those who continue to watch television when the broadcasters are on strike.
The phantom limb which goes on hurting even after it is amputated.
The man who is made redundant but goes regularly to his former place of work every morning.
The Japanese stubbornly contemplating the sunset at Ayer's Rock even though there is no sun.
The tightrope-walker who keeps edging forward on his imaginary rope until he realizes it is not there and falls into the void.
The subject who takes himself for a subject even though he disappeared long ago.

The repentant, run-to-seed ultra-Leftists who have converted to humanitarianism, artificial inseminators of the widow and the orphan, themselves orphans of reality and *malades imaginaires* of politics, premature ejaculators of posthistory and hyperchondriacs [*hypercondriaques*] of the dead body of ideology and morality.

Annoyed at having first to turn his pullovers the right side out every time he puts them on, he decides to turn them around as soon as he has taken them off. Surely, this is rational. But since this decision does not override the decision automatically to turn out his pullover when he puts it on, he unfailingly ends up with it the wrong side out. A dilemma: how is one to rationalize an act without disturbing one's automatic behaviour? And things are even worse if, faced with this failure, one resolves to give up the innovation, since the old practice is then immediately disrupted too, being no longer spontaneous and infallible. The situation created is a hopeless tangle. The lesson of all this: all clothing should be reversible. Ideas, too, so that one could slip into them from any side.

The mute orgasm of the smile.

The strategy of idleness – that is to say, the unshakeable desire to escape the violation of our time by all kinds of predatory, futile activities – consists in putting off the point where those activities have to be done, spacing them so that they can be picked off one by one, as in the story of the Horatii and Curiatii. The other form of idleness is impatience; it is finishing before we have started – which is a way of coming out free on the other side. *Expectare, diluere, suspendere humanum est . . .*

Every scrambled image (Canal+ without the decoder) immediately takes on an erotic charge.[22] The imagination, which cannot give itself free rein, automatically begins to fantasize in that direction. And the encrypted verbal exchanges merely heighten the viewer's onanism. *Porno sfumato* is, in the end, much more erotic than the message 'in clear'. More generally, every clear signification is anti-erotic.

Seeing things from beyond their end – as transfinite, so to speak. They appear in an entirely different light. Events come to you from the opposite direction in time, from the depths of their past occurrence.

It is the same with concepts in theory: you see them coming from another direction than that of their logical unfolding – from the depths of their accomplishment, which is also their end, as in a film run backwards.

One should always maintain a kind of balance in this way between a thing and its extreme final term, hold the two simultaneously in tension. Thus, we must live both with the system and with the extreme consequences of the system.

Only once the different realms, sexes, races and species have ceased to be incomparable and have begun to evaluate their difference on a common scale, only then can they measure themselves one against the other, and gain an advantage over each other.

The modern theory of evolution played a crucial role here.

There is no scale of measure in the symbolic chain. No species is inferior to any other. Nor is any human being. All that counts is the symbolic sequence. It is only when they have become autonomous and distinct (have been 'liberated') that they become different and thus automatically inferior or superior to one another. It is out of the move to a universal stand- ard of measure based on 'objective' criteria that all forms of discrimination arise.

Dangerous un-liaisons.

Implacable un-liaison from the dead mother. Implacable deliverance, which one will have to expiate by an inner sacrifice – a sudden void which will have to be filled by a secret amassing of guilt. For successful mourning is always the equivalent of a virtual murder of the dead person, and the work of mourning is not a deliverance in itself, but the price paid for liberation.

And it is not just the living who perform their work of mourning; the dead also must do so. They have to give up the living in order to be really dead, just as the living have to give up the dead in order to be really alive. And this is no easier for the dead than it is for the living. Some refuse to do this, or do not achieve it: they then have to continue persecuting the living, just as the living sometimes have nothing better to do than persecute their dead, or persecute themselves in the name of their dead. Without reciprocal, agreed separation we have the twilight state of the living dead.

Why remonstrate against the current deliquescence and senility of the political class? As though we still believed we were governed by intelligent people when it is glaringly obvious that we are convinced of the opposite. We ought, rather, to whoop for joy: all that we anticipated has come to pass, with the collusion of the political class itself! It is that class, in all its political colorations, which is currently carrying out the *fatwa*, the decree of dissolution and disappearance we had pronounced on it – we, the theorists of the shadows, the mirror peoples. We are thus torn between registering this catastrophic state of fact, unable not to share in the collective shame of it, and a secret jubilation at this decomposition foretold. We have, moreover, to congratulate Mitterrand on accomplishing the task we dreamed of: of having made certain, by a kind of posthumous clearing of the decks, of the deep-seated corruption of the whole political system, of having mystified and swept away the whole of the divine Left!

Gut reaction against yobbery, the masses and solid Frenchness. But an equally visceral distaste for the elite, for castes, culture and the *nomenklatura*. Do we have to choose between the moronic masses and the arrogant privileged classes (particularly when they have an odour of demagogic humility about them)? No solution.

Islamic fundamentalism – a providential target for a system which no longer knows what values to subscribe to – has a pendant in Western integrism, the integrism of the universal and of forced democracy, which is equally intolerant, since it, too, does not grant the other the moral and political right to exist.

This is free-market fanaticism, the fanaticism of indifference to its own values and, for that very reason, total intolerance towards those who differ by any passion whatsoever. The New World Order implies the extermination of everything different to integrate it into an indifferent world order.

Is there still room between these two fanaticisms for a non-believer to exercise his liberty?

The students mount a demonstration and hold up the TGV in Angoulême station. They flow around both sides of the train, alongside the passengers, who remain immobile behind their tinted windows. There are some shouts and slogans, a few cries of rage – but against whom? It is as though, thinking to howl at the moon, they were barking at an artificial satellite. In fact, they are barking at the TGV as though at virtual reality on its passage. For the TGV is virtual reality crossing France *in vitro* – an incarnation of speed, money, and all that circulates, now confronted with their real world of potential unemployment. A surrealist confrontation between time's arrow and a youth already spent.

All they will get from the transparency of the rich is this ten minutes of immobility, ten minutes of freeze-frame in the television show of which they are the victims. And they unwittingly make a present of these ten minutes to the rootless speed freaks: a moment of accidental respite, moments of immobility and silence snatched back from the apocalyptic, fanatical passion for motion, moments we find now only in strikes and blockades.

The newly discovered Combe d'Arc cave is too good to be true. It was immediately closed up, and since no one will ever be let in, it might as well never have existed. The need to protect the paintings is a legitimate one, but it coincides too neatly with our exile in the Virtual and our definitive distancing from the Real. Cave paintings and fossilized remains are becoming like invisible gold reserves, sealed away and shielded from reality. In this way, they no longer even need to exist exactly, and their very existence becomes a matter of some doubt. On the other hand, their growth – and the growth in the number of archaeological discoveries – is inevitable. It is entirely as though such deposits were being invented as the need for them arises. It is much the same with material consumer goods. As soon as demand exceeds supply (and the collective frenzy for origins, the almost instinctual demand for discovering tracks, has grown enormous) everything pitches over into simulation, into the forced production of signs, with the rate of credibility in free fall.

We 'discovered' primitive societies, America, the atom, the unconscious, viruses. But the consequences of this expansion of the field of knowledge escape us. We believe we discovered these things innocently in the peaceful realm of science. But they, too, discovered us and have broken in on our world – just deserts for our breaking in on theirs.

The atom's revenge has been striking. And that of viruses is no less blatant. The revenge of the savages, deep-lying, lurks in wait for us, with those of all the mirror people we have disturbed in their otherness and with their secrets.

Did they exist before we 'discovered' them? Did the Unconscious exist before it was discovered? Nothing could be less certain. But, deep down, this unanswerable question is unimportant. The main thing is that, once they have been discovered, these objects are never again content merely to exist as objects of knowledge or analysis: they react in an original, offensive way, and we may fall prey to – or be taken hostage by – them. Even when they are hounded, domesticated, pacified or obliterated, they pass into our whole arterial and cultural system as filterable viruses. To the revenge of the mirror peoples is added that of the beings on this side of the mirror, on this side of all representation and resemblance, those molecular beings which live in intangible, infinitesimal realms – virtual beings from elsewhere, from the depths of the genome, of the clone, of microbiology, which are the infra-human equivalent of what has emerged from the depths of primitive cultures and has slowly devastated Western culture. Beings even more primitive than savages will come from the other side of the mirror, where they have until now been contained – enough 'Aliens'[23] to cripple the human race in its entirety. There is no alternative. We cannot but discover them and 'liberate' them and they cannot but destroy us. The whole process is what it is; it is a kind of fate. How could one not be destroyed by what one discovers – for better or for worse? How could one not destroy it, by the very fact of discovering it?

Let us not underestimate, either, the object's (malicious) desire to be discovered. There can be no doubt that, once a window opens up in the field of knowledge, phenomena rush to be hastily discovered and decoded. Perhaps they even compete to be decoded ahead of some other pheno-menon. In this same way, some humans manage to get themselves loved in some other person's stead, taking advantage of an opening not intended for them.

The mass as the elusive variable in all social equations. The mass intangible and undetectable, but constituting the density of the social. The dark matter of power, that critical mass which causes it to implode by its very extension.

The incalculable mass of the events which do not take place and which create a kind of historical anti-gravity, altering the trajectory and meaning of the events which do. A secret mass everywhere defies the visible equations, knocks them out of kilter, yet obscurely maintains the density, coherence and gravitation of the whole.

If this dark matter did not exist, our 'material' universe would long since have vanished into thin air. Moreover, if we succeeded in eliminating it, there is nothing to suggest that this would not be the most probable outcome.

Wherever this dark matter, this void, this parallel universe, this inverse energy, this antagonistic principle, this radical illusion, disappears, the real immediately meets with catastrophe. The real purged of the anti-real becomes hyperreal. It becomes more real than the real, and collapses into itself. Matter purged of anti-matter is doomed to entropy. The elimination of the void causes matter to collapse into itself.

The subject, stripped of all otherness, collapses into itself. The elimination of the inhuman causes the human to collapse into odium and ridicule.

But the question remains: why do we wish to hunt out this void? Why this phantasy of expelling the dark matter, of making everything visible, of realizing everything, of forcibly expressing that which does not desire expression? Of exhuming that Nothing which alone ensured the continuity of the secret? Why is this positivity at all costs so lethally tempting?

An insoluble question. But perhaps this move to get to the bottom of all that is secret itself has a secret aim?

With regard to mass and the masses, we should speak, rather, of a critical frequency.

Of information, for example, in which field it seems we are doing all we can to get beyond that frequency, that critical threshold of planetary information, of universal instantaneity of information, which will automatically bring about a violent contraction, a Big Crunch. It may be that this is our dream. Not being sure of seeing its effects at the cosmic level, we are tempted to set it in train in an apocalyptic register more on our own scale by intensifying the universal process of information-generation to the point of producing that famous phase inversion which would give us an experimental facsimile of the catastrophic end of the universe.

Conventional science bases itself on a single negative experiment to disqualify all the others (the case of Jacques Benveniste). Now, the movement of a science 'in progress' is exactly the opposite: a single extraordinary fact, a single exceptional experiment, is sufficient to throw into question the whole conventional edifice of science. It is sufficient for water, just once, to have shown evidence of memory. . .

It is the same with reality. It takes just one single anomic, enigmatic fact to throw the conventional picture into doubt. The exception does not prove the rule; it disproves the rule. Yet we also need to know where the exception lies. In the moral order, it is evil that is the exception: a single tragic event (the death of a child – Dostoevsky) throws the order of the world into question. But why not take the view that the fundamental rule is that of evil, and that any happy event throws it into question? Is not true optimism to consider the world a fundamentally negative event, with many happy exceptions? By contrast, does not true pessimism consist in viewing the world as fundamentally good, leaving the slightest accident to make us despair of that vision? An ideal universe at the mercy of the slightest reverse and doomed, in any case, to death? And does not true superstition consist in regarding evil as an exception which ought to disappear?

We judge everything today in terms of a real and rational sequence of events. But we could equally fully and reasonably view those events as part of an irrational sequence – we simply have to reverse the perspective and take a maleficent transcendence rather than a providential force as our reference. We would be less despairing if we regarded every misfortune as justified by a transcendent order of evil.

Such is the rule of a radical optimism. We must make evil the basic rule. Then, the fortunate occurrence becomes the exception. Then, it is joy we would be fated to meet with. At any rate, in relation to an impossible truth, the two hypotheses are equally (im)plausible. But the hypothesis of evil has the advantage of restoring to the world its illegal character. Moreover, it lends a new prestige to good and happiness, the prestige of a miraculous exception.

The wonderful final scene of *Jurassic Park*, in which the cloned neo-dinosaurs wreck the museum and wreak havoc upon their fossilized ancestors – quite a good anticipation of the fate of our own species, trapped between its fossils and its clones.

The problem of the human species is that we are beginning to have seen it all already, and are even starting to feel this ourselves. Given humanity's virtual mastery of the world and its total(?) success as a species, it is no longer its evolution but its disappearance that is becoming interesting. It is at this point that the dinosaurs are celebrating their sensational comeback. We are using the dinosaurs to flirt with our own abolition as a species. We are projecting ourselves into the past in the form of the only species whose domination was as total as ours, and which has spectacularly disappeared.

We know species are mortal; but we have never really envisaged this for our own, being persuaded not only that we are the last, but also that our power gives us immunity. Now, instead of fantasizing about external catastrophes, cosmic, seismic or climatic, we might ask ourselves whether the dinosaurs did not disappear as a result of a catastrophic internal process – precisely on account of that maximum power and its reversal, as all systems reverse at their apogee. There is nothing to say we are not mentally and biologically programmed for an internal disappearance of the same order, as the logical consequence of our power. There is nothing to say this disappearance has not been our dream. In any event, we are joyfully collaborating in it.

Thus, in a sense, the dinosaurs are our model of disappearance in the past. But we have another one in the future. We are using automata and clones to flirt with the technical immortality which equates just as much to our disappearance as a species. The genetic transfiguring of the species, the technical counterfeiting of the world, the innumerable artificial devices yet to come, are our hypostasis in the future, in a virtual dimension which might be that of the end of the millennium (and perhaps even the end of the Quaternary). It is our disappearance into the virtual that we are currently playing out in real time. In other words, we no longer even perceive ourselves, since, with the assistance of the evil genius of computers, the memory of the process erases itself automatically. Virtual beings are already here. Like the dinosaurs in the museum who fall victim to their clones, we are already fossils prey to virtual beings. But seen in terms of Gosse's simultaneously naive and malicious hypothesis, this final scene in *Jurassic Park* is even more extraordinary since, on his account, the fossilized dinosaurs are already clones, artificial beings born of the a posteriori simulation by God of the genesis of species.

Sociology, semiology, Marxism, psychoanalysis – all this is part of the spoils. The specialists in the various disciplines are sharing out the spoils of a world in decay. Spoil system. The unemployed and social workers share out the spoils of a decaying social labour-power. Experts in digital abstraction share out the spoils of a reality in distress. Thus proliferate the defrocked priests of meaning, the defrocked priests of labour, the defrocked priests of reality.

Suicide might be said to be the perfect crime in that murderer and victim are one. But basically, this is merely a particular case of a more general rule which is the essence of crime, as it is of any passion or extreme situation: the rule that object and subject are merged.

The distinction between subject and object is much more commonly the exception.

Have I actually wiped away all the traces, all the possible consequences of this book? Did I reach a point where nothing can be made of it; did I abolish every last desire to give it a meaning? Have I achieved that continuity of the Nothing? In that case, I have succeeded. I have done to the book what the system has done to reality: turned it into something no one knows what to do with any more. But something they don't know how to get rid of either.

Covering your own tracks makes you a criminal, even if you have nothing to blame yourself for.

There is no corpse of the real, and with good reason: the real is not dead, it has disappeared.

If the book finishes off reality, the way they finish off horses (they shoot them, don't they?), the reality of the book remains none the less. If information kills the event, the reality of information remains. Yes, but that reality of information is virtual. And where the reality of the book is concerned, is that actually a reality? The book is neither a real object nor a virtual one. It submits to no protocol of verification. It is in this sense alone that it is necessary. In present times, there is an absolute need for a book, for a non-identifiable object, an absolute need to revive anything whatever – act, word, face, landscape, event or catastrophe – which eludes both the real and the virtual.

Art was the poetic transfiguration of the real. Philosophy was the poetic transfiguration of the concept. What must henceforth be transfigured is the disappearance of all those things – the real, the concept, art, nature, and philosophy itself.

The crime would like to give itself away without ceasing to be perfect – that is to say, invisible. Similarly, the book would like to make itself heard without ceasing to have nothing to say. Everything dreams in this way of transfiguring itself into its opposite without ceasing to be itself. Even good and evil dream of each other from the depths of their loneliness.

In the past, the aim was to commit crimes without their being discovered. Today, crimes are concerned not so much with being committed as with being discovered. On occasion, they invent their own clues. This is the exact opposite of the perfect crime.

Circular rule of three between the book, the crime and perfection. If the book is not perfect, it will not be the equivalent of the crime it is attempting to describe. It will be perfect only if it is itself criminal. But the crime, for its part, would not be perfect without the book: it is not perfect in itself. And it is because it is not perfect that there can be a book. There is no untangling this sequence.

This book, which stands out against perfection, simultaneously sees to it that it never gets caught out. This is perfectly contradictory. Contravening the basic rule, it plays neither on reality nor on truth, but on self-evidence. It claims to be quite simply self-evident, and it is on this account that it sinks almost involuntarily into perfection.

He does not have room both for the world and for its double – but no one knows which will have the last word.

In view of the objective non-meaning that is the world's, all our little subjective impulses towards non-meaning, our pathetic desire for non-meaning, seem quite laughable.

The self-evidence of the real is as unacceptable as the state of political affairs.

The self-evidence of facts is just as unacceptable as injustice or poverty.

The scandal of reality, of the legality of the real, is equal to the scandal of the moral law and the official order.

The state of things is precisely what it is only because reality, the superstition of reality, plays a primordial role in it.

One cannot, then, change anything in political reality without striking at reality itself.

Why is it that at the very heart of chaos some indomitable elective affinities manifest themselves? These are the strange attractors.

But why is it that at the very heart of order indomitable repulsions, indomitable negative reactions, also appear? These are the strange detractors.

The advantage of being happy is that one is rid of the question of happiness. The advantage of being free is that one is rid of the question of freedom.

It is at this point that everything begins: when the concepts which existed only as questions appear as answers. It is the end of the cycle and the beginning of a new turning point: how can we rediscover the question behind the answer – how can we rediscover, behind happiness, the idea of happiness?

Four vital functions, as basic as the four elements: sexuality, sociality, ideation and glory. Or: pleasure, speech, thought and prestige.

Being deprived of any of the four leads to stupor and death.

It is impatience which makes me grasp so poorly what others say in a foreign language. It is hurriedness to understand which means that I do not even listen to them. But I speak all the more freely for this.

Thus, I express myself all the better for not managing to communicate, I write all the better for not managing to speak, I think all the better for not managing to write.

The mass is the social equivalent of the perfect crime, since it is without subject or object, has no message for no addressee, leaves no trace and has no motive. And if it is without ultimate goal and without desire, this is because it is, all at once, its own subject, its own object, its own material and its own author (J.-P. Curnier).

Pox and fudge (on current society).

He says: 'I fucked her.'
She says: 'I fucked with him.'
In the one case (the man), the verb is transitive – it has an object. In the other (the woman), it is intransitive – it has an instrument. Which proves there is no sexual relation – as the Man said.

She can also say, 'I got myself fucked.' Which is not so much passive as factitive, for if she is the passive object of 'fucked', she is the active subject of 'got'. It is she who gets (herself) fucked. This is, so to speak, the middle voice which indicates that the action relates to oneself, is done for oneself and to one's advantage. To all this we should oppose the duel, in sexual as well as grammatical terms: neither subject nor object, neither active nor passive, neither singular nor plural. This takes us beyond all oppositions of gender, number and mood – the only solution to the sexual and social question.

Some women have orgasms without knowing it. Some simulate orgasm without having one (but doubtless end up finding their pleasure in the simulacrum). Uncertainty as to the female orgasm is at the heart of the sexual illusion. Women make do with this situation quite well, and can content themselves with play rather than pleasure – all the more so as, in the order of physical pleasure, true and false no longer have any definition. Whereas man is real, having to deal with the reality of his erection and hardly being able to simulate that effect (desire, for its part, can merely be virtual, but the erection is real) – woman is less linked to any reality whatsoever, except to that of her partner. She is, therefore, closer to illusion, play and simulation. Sexual pleasure itself is certainly engendered – and heightened – by the fact that man and woman do not have the same status of reality. But this is also the reason why there is no sexual relation.

Against the 'objective' analysis of an 'objective' state of affairs (the stupidity of sociology!), it must be seen that we think and speak well only of what we have not experienced – that is to say, of what we have not exhausted the imagining of by lived experience – just as one truly loves a woman only if one has not exhausted one's imagining of her in physical pleasure.

Every real idea of an object involves the denial of its reality, its abstraction – not the abstraction of method, but the abstracting of the object itself – and thus a transobjectal form which scorns objectivity. In this sense, all thought is an imposture. It speaks of what it is not. This is the Great Game. If I speak of the game without being a player, then that precisely is play, a game, and in precisely that respect I am a player (who will never be bigger than the game itself).

The very fact of having to defend the historical reality of the gas chambers as a moral cause, the fact of having to defend 'reality' by a kind of political commitment, is adequate testimony to the change of register of historical truth and the troubles of objectivity. The problem is: why is there even a need to speak up for truth against the negationists, and why can their question even be put (it never could have been in any other age)?

The negationists' proposition is interesting if one allows oneself to consider it, and is not merely content to reject it with indignation. Where the negationists are absolutely wrong is when they contest the historical reality of the Holocaust. The event took place in historical time and the proof is there. But we are not now in historical time, but in real time, and in real time there is no longer any proof of anything whatever – the Holocaust will never be verified in real time. Negationism is, therefore, absurd in its own logic, but, by its very absurdity, it throws light on the irruption of another dimension, another kind of time, which is paradoxically called real time but in which it is precisely objective reality which disappears – and not just the reality of the present event but that of the past event and, equally, of the future event – while exhausting itself in an instantaneity such that no act or event can find any real cause or continuation. In that real time, history can no longer be reflected. Real time is a kind of black hole into which nothing can penetrate without being desubstantialized. In real time, the extermination camps become virtual and appear only on the screen of virtuality, and all the testimonies and Holocaust and Shoah sink, in spite of themselves and in spite of us, into the same virtual abyss – that of the images and facts which exist for as long as they exist, and that is all. It is not clear that, in their absolute sincerity, the testimonies themselves and the films do not contribute to this impossible memory. The real extermination is doomed to this other extermination which is that effected by the virtual. This is the true final solution.

The negationist proposition, in the age in which it is being advanced, cannot therefore be truly denied, since everything, all of us, including those who reject it, have passed over, whether we like it or not, into an age where there is no longer any objective recourse. The proposition, therefore, can be rejected only by a kind of mirror denial. And that is where its victory lies – though in fact it is not *its* victory, but the victory of real time over the present, over the past, over any form whatsoever of logical articulation of reality.

Nor is the future sure of its existence in real time (this was the sense of 'The Year 2000 will not take place'[24]). We come back to Berkeley's hypothesis of creation being entirely renewed at every moment by God – otherwise, continuity disappears and the world falls apart: nothing makes any sense a moment later. This is pretty much how things are with real time.

Where are the songs of Hölderlin, the gentle slopes beside the Neckar?
'Jetzt aber sitz' ich unter Wolken (deren
Ein jedes eine Ruh' hat eigen) . . .'
The Gods have been chased away. Their spectres hover about the deserts of postmodernity. If it took place anywhere, surely the perfect crime had its embodiment here.
'. . . und fremd erscheinen und
gestorben mir
der Seeligen Geister.'

As I speak, there floats over the auditorium, rather like an ectoplasmic shade, the fog of incomprehension which emanates from the brains present, like the mist of breath rising from cattle in the early morning. A cerebral breath you could cut with a knife, through which words, with the aid of forceps, force a path towards paradox.

This statue in the Luxembourg Gardens which I find infinitely seductive. It is the statue of a naked girl, reclining against an obelisk and delicately holding in her left hand a strange object elegantly directed towards her nubile sex – the whole doubtless celebrating the Alsatian benefactor of humanity whose bas-relief portrait adorns the base, offering an allegorical mix of candour and obscenity characteristic of *fin-de-siècle* sculptural academicism. Well, this young statue – which I see repeatedly on my walks through the gardens and which still gives me as much pleasure as ever – seemed to me the other day to have changed physically. She seemed to have put on weight; she didn't seem quite so prepubescent and she seemed to have stopped washing: she looked slovenly. Is she perhaps reaching puberty before my very eyes (I am the only person who looks at her)? The mystery of statues, which we presume to be indifferent to their own bodies. This one, as she becomes a woman, will perhaps begin to bleed? Whence perhaps the utility of that strange object she is holding between her slender fingers. And this Doctor 'Kreisler' . . . Was he the inventor of the Tampax, perhaps, or of the dildo?

Very gradually, sexual life comes to an end the way it began. Having awakened first to dreams before coming to reality, it is in the end returning to the fantasy, to the imagining of the first sexual objects – like the fetishism connected with the first arousals in one's immediate milieu.

Since one spends one's time earning the right to live, why not do this by an immersion in icy water, after which one can enjoy a lasciviousness without compunction? Baptism by cold, the early-morning sacrifice of the body, provides absolution for the whole day.

At the foot of these karstic cliffs, in this gorge with its sarcastic freshness, the tourist authorities have installed their marble seats, their concrete shroud, their picnic tables – all the signs of urban infamy and a prostitution of space.

The serenity and unserenity which absolution from all conflict, from all worldly rivalry, brings. It is precisely in this serene margin from which all causes of anxiety have been banished that one finds welling up, at the outer limits of a perfect – and hence criminal – tranquillity, an opposite anxiety – an anxiety which is not psychodegradable, is irrational and instinctual, and comes not from the psychical unconscious but from the body, from one's biological heritage, and can be appeased only by tiring that body out.

The Cathars, who are now virtually as vanished as the dinosaurs, are also re-emerging like clones in the museums, on the tourist routes, in the restored castles, in the computerized archives and lastly, no doubt, in the Cathar DNA molecules taken from fossilized skeletons: starting out from a fragment of their genetic code, Cathars will be reconstructed just like dinosaurs or bacteria. The destiny of all that has disappeared is *Jurassic Park*.

In this land of perpetual wind and drought, the silent humidity is an event when all the elements are merged in an indistinct, hepatic luminosity, instead of the clarity of light which usually prevails. All the winds have dropped, and the fire of the sky is shrouded in mist. You can no longer even hear the grass growing, as you are said to do in legend. An autumn day in the middle of summer, a day which never broke and lasts for an eternity: until ten o'clock at night.

As the day declines, night also *falls*. Is this not strange? There is a nonsensicality here which ought to alert us to the semantic disorder of language.

Why has the night not the right to break like the day? (there is also no term to describe its end). Yet it does break. Some nights, you see it breaking, growing on the horizon, invading space like a shining star, in an ascending movement rising up from the earth. And objects, letting their light gradually slip away, themselves emerge into a new form, into their nocturnal essence. But, for us, neither the night nor evil has an essence of its own.

Continental Divide.

Somewhere in Colorado, the mysterious demarcation line where the waters part – flowing off towards the Atlantic on the one hand, and to the Pacific on the other. A line which is, in fact, every bit as imaginary as the one separating the future from the past – a line we call the present, the two dimensions of time also streaming away into other oceanic depths.

In man, it is thoughts, not rivers, which divide. Like the continental waters, they run off subtly and quite unpredictably in opposite directions, to disappear in any event into some impersonal ocean. Thus those ideas whose sources are the closest will end up furthest from each other.

It is along the same imaginary line, the same invisible crest, that Left and Right, man and woman, good and evil, and all languages separate for ever.

Though there is no centre of the world, there is always at the origin this demarcation line traced out by nature, which creates by this something more than a difference: a definitive divergence. This means that, at a particular moment, not only do things separate, but, like the constellations of signs or those in space, they go on endlessly moving apart – the tension between them diminishing to infinity until it reaches oceanic indifference.

Just as the waters, coming from the same sky and the same rains, part, so the fates of men, coming from the same primal scene, take a different course. But perhaps they meet up again somewhere, just like the meridians which seem to diverge at one pole only the better to converge again at the other.

For our part, on either side of an imaginary line of the will, every decision creates two opposing slopes on which life will flow off in opposite directions – each fraction of destiny moving irremediably away from the other. But each personal destiny, like rain and clouds, will scatter out again into the impersonal cycle. As for time, each moment is the dividing line where past and future separate, never to meet again. Moreover, existence is merely the ever greater divergence between past and future until death unites the two in an absolute present.

The parting of the waters, then, is always a paradoxical distancing like that between mountain peaks: the highest peaks – though they are, being the highest, the furthest from each other – are also the closest.

In a single continent, itself half unreal, the waters do not diverge but, rather, converge towards the centre to run away into the same desert: Australia. The symbol of a world where division has not taken place: a lethal, foetal, involutive world in which the waters, the animals (marsupials) and the humans (dreamtime) go back to their sources rather than running their course, collapse into their primal scenes rather than meeting their ends. The antipodal universe of dreams.

Keep objects as a system
Keep production as a mirror
Keep death as an exchange
Keep the world as a simulacrum

Keep the evil transparent
Keep the majorities silent
Keep your seduction alive
Keep your memory cool

Keep yourself as an other
Keep perfection as a crime
Keep illusion for the end
Keep on line for the while[25]

NOTES

1. Antoine-Léonard Thomas (1732–85), 'Ode sur le temps'.
2. 'Be careful!' is in English in the original.
3. Les Humanoïdes Associés are Paris-based publishers, largely of adult comic books.
4. Text of advertisements in English in the original.
5. Kawabata, *House of the Sleeping Beauties and Other Stories*, trans. Edward G. Seidensticker, The Quadriga Press, London 1969, p. 39.
6. A reference to Antoine Houdar de Lamotte's famous line 'L'ennui naquit un jour de l'uniformité', 'Les amis trop d'accord', *Fables*, 1719.
7. The French here is 'la fin de l'Empire du Sens, de l'Empire des Signes'. The French 'empire sur' has the banal, everyday sense of 'hold' or 'sway' over something, but Baudrillard's reference to 'l'Empire du Sens' is also perhaps an allusion to the Japanese film *Ai no corrida* (Empire of the Senses).
8. This paragraph is entirely in English in the original.
9. The acts and opinions of Alfred Jarry's pataphysician Dr Faustroll were first recorded in an *édition hors commerce* of 1898.
10. 'Perdu de vue', presented by Jacques Pradel, is a long-running 'magazine programme', based on the idea of tracing missing persons, on the French television channel TF1.
11. These are located on the coast of Brittany.
12. In English in the original.

13. Legend has it that the two recumbent figures in the museum of the abbey of Jumièges are likenesses of the sons of Clovis II, who, as punishment for a revolt against their father, had the tendons of their arms and legs cut and were set adrift in a boat on the Seine.
14. The normal English usage here is, of course, a 'shred of proof', a 'ghost of a chance'.
15. To be precise here, the French term *ordure* implies a level of moral turpitude not conveyed in the English.
16. John Updike, *Rabbit at Rest*, André Deutsch, London 1990, p. 267.
17. In English in the original.
18. Baltasar Gracián (1601–58), Spanish writer and philosopher.
19. 'Answer to the Question: "What is Enlightenment?"', in *Political Writings*, ed. Hans Reiss, Cambridge University Press, second edition, 1991, p. 54.
20. The Tasaday are an isolated people who were discovered apparently leading a Stone Age existence in the highland rainforest of Mindanao by Western anthropologists in 1971. The government of the Philippines susequently made extensive provision for their 'preservation'.
21. *Il mondo senza donne* is a novel by Virgilio Martini.
22. Canal+ is a French-language subscription television channel.
23. The reference here is to the creatures in Ridley Scott's film *Alien*.
24. Presumably an illusion to Baudrillard's own paper 'L'An 2000 ne passera pas', which first appeared in *Traverses* 32, 1985 (pp. 15–17).
25. In English in the original.